THEMATIC UNIT
Pasta and Pizza

Written By Cindy Holzschuher

Teacher Created Materials

Teacher Created Materials, Inc.
6421 Industry Way
Westminster, CA 92683
www.teachercreated.com
©1999 Teacher Created Materials, Inc.
Made in U.S.A.

ISBN-1-57690-374-5

Contributing Editor
Janet A. Hale, M.S. Ed.

Illustrated by
Larry Bauer

Cover Art by
Agi Palinay

Table of Contents

Introduction

Pasta and Pizza is a complete thematic unit focusing on two favorite foods of children around the world. It contains 80 pages of lesson ideas and reproducible activities. At its core are two pieces of high-quality children's literature, *Strega Nona*, by Tomie dePaola, and *Pasta*, by Kate Haycock, as well as a reproducible book, *Pizza Fit for a Queen*. Across the curriculum ideas are included which set the stage for learning, encourage the enjoyment of the book, and extend the concepts gained. You will find activities and practice sheets for language arts, math, social studies, science, art, music, and life skills. Many of the suggested activities encourage cooperative learning. Ideas for bulletin boards, learning centers, and awards are unit management tools that can help the busy teacher. The culminating activities will allow the children to synthesize their knowledge and provide an opportunity to share this knowledge with others.

This thematic unit includes:

❑ **literature selections**—summaries of two children's books and an original story with related lessons and suggestions for pre-reading, reading, and post-reading activities

❑ **writing and language experience ideas**—daily suggestions as well as writing activities that span across the curriculum

❑ **poetry**—related to the unit topics

❑ **planning guides**—suggestions for your lesson planning

❑ **curriculum connections**—in language arts, math, social studies, science, art, music, and life skills

❑ **bulletin board suggestions**—for displaying children's work and their gained knowledge

❑ **culminating activities**—that require children to synthesize their learning by engaging in activities that can be shared with others

❑ **a bibliography**—suggests literature as well as other helpful resources for materials related to the theme

To keep this valuable resource intact so that it can be used year after year, you may wish to punch holes in the pages and store them in a three-ring binder.

Introduction *(cont.)*

Why A Balanced Approach?

The strength of a balanced language approach is that it involves children in using all modes of communication—reading, writing, listening, illustrating, and doing. Communication skills are interconnected and integrated into lessons that emphasize the whole of language. Implicit in this approach is our knowledge that every whole—including individual words—is composed of parts, and directed study of those parts can help a child to master the whole. Experience and research tell us that regular attention to phonics, other word attack skills, spelling, etc., develops reading mastery, thereby fulfilling the unity of the whole language experience. The child is thus led to read, write, spell, speak, and listen more confidently.

Why Thematic Planning?

One very useful tool for implementing an integrated language program is thematic planning. By choosing a theme with a correlating literature selection for a unit of study, a teacher can plan activities throughout the day that lead to a cohesive, in-depth study of the topic. Children will be practicing and applying their skills in meaningful context. Consequently, they tend to learn and retain more.

Why Cooperative Learning?

Besides academic skills and content, children need to learn social skills. No longer can this area of development be taken for granted. Children must learn to work cooperatively in groups in order to function well in modern society. Group activities should be a regular part of school life, and teachers should consciously include social objectives as well as academic objectives in their planning.

Why Big Books?

An excellent cooperative, whole language activity is the production of big books. Groups of children, or the whole class, can apply their language skills, content knowledge, and creativity to produce a big book that becomes a part of the classroom library to be read and reread. These books make excellent culminating projects for sharing beyond the classroom with parents, librarians, other classes, etc.

Why Journals?

Each day your children should have the opportunity to write in a journal. They may respond to a book or an event in history, write about a personal experience, or answer a general "question of the day" posed by the teacher. The cumulative journal provides an excellent means of documenting children's writing progress.

Strega Nona

by Tomie dePaola

Summary

Strega Nona hires Big Anthony to help her with household chores. When she leaves home for the day, curious Anthony repeats a rhyme he heard her saying that starts her magic pasta pot boiling. Unfortunately, he does not know how to make it stop! By the time Strega Nona returns, the town is flooded with pasta. Big Anthony then learns a very "filling" lesson.

The outline below is a suggested plan for using the various activities presented in this unit.

Sample Plan

Lesson I

- Familiarize your children with the country of Italy (page 6, Setting the Stage, #3).

- Make Italian Flags (page 56).

- Survey who has eaten pasta lately (page 6, Setting the Stage, #4).

- Read *Strega Nona.*

- Create Help Wanted posters (page 6, Enjoying the Book, #3).

- Make Strega Nona's Pasta Pots (page 11).

- Italian dishes use herbs for flavoring. Try Using Your Head (page 49) for a herb smelling and tasting experience.

Lesson II

- Retell *Strega Nona* by drawing mini-scenes (page 7, #1).

- Look through the *Strega Nona* illustrations until you find the ones that show the town covered with noodles. Make Big Anthony's Pasta Pot flip books (page 9).

- Conduct a yellow "pasta" yarn measuring activity (page 6, Enjoying the Book, #2).

- Complete Is it Time to Eat? (page 43).

- Create Dancing Noodle Necklaces (page 62).

Lesson III

- Look through the *Strega Nona* illustrations until you find the one that shows Big Anthony blowing two kisses. What would have happened if he had blown three kisses (page 7, #3)?

- Read, or have the children read, the Family Favorite poem (page 29).

- Prepare and eat a packaged or canned spaghetti treat.

- Create Pasta Patterns (page 38).

- Make Spaghetti Name Tags (page 55).

Lesson IV

- Learn more about the personal lives of Strega Nona and Big Anthony (page 7, #4).

- Have the children draw pictures of a young Big Anthony and young Strega Nona; display.

- Try Painting with Pasta (page 57).

- How many words can your children make from the word SPAGHETTI (page 7, #8)?

Overview of Activities

Setting the Stage

1. To help you gain background knowledge about pasta and pizza, visit the Web sites listed on page 63, as well as reading pages 19, 44, 48, 50–54, and 79.

2. Create the bulletin-board display entitled An Italian Look (page 70), as well as one or all of the learning centers (pages 72–73) to spark an interest in your children for learning about pasta and pizza. An excellent, additional visual aid would be to post travel posters on your walls and place brochures on trips to Italy in the reading learning center area (posters and brochures are available at most travel agencies).

3. Point out Italy on the prepared bulletin board (see #2 above). Locate the capital, Rome, and the town in which the story *Strega Nona* takes place, Calabria. Calabria is a sea-coast town in the southern region of Italy. It is known for its beauty and easy lifestyle; therefore, the Calabria region, as well as the city of Calabria itself, attracts tourists who want a leisurely holiday. You may want to complete That's an Italian Fact! (page 54) as a group, referring back to the map as you complete the activity.

4. With your children, brainstorm a list of ways that people eat pasta (in salads, soups, lasagne, etc.). Take a survey to find how many of your children have eaten pasta in the last 24 hours, last week, and last month. Show the children a variety of pasta shapes. Which of the shapes have they eaten? Conduct a second survey to see which types of pasta they have eaten the most of and which they have eaten the least of.

Enjoying the Book

1. Create a pasta exploration area in your room complete with ladles or large spoons, tablespoons, teaspoons, a set of measuring cups, several sizes of bowls, pasta pots, and a few pounds (kilos) of a variety of dry pastas. Allow the children to create "pretend" recipes by using the measuring devices and pouring the pasta into the bowls and pasta pots. This activity allows the children to freely explore the concept of volume.

2. Prepare a large bowl of different lengths of yellow yarn "spaghetti" for practicing measurement. Encourage the children to compare the various "spaghetti" lengths using rulers, as well as measuring various items in the room using a 6" (15 cm) or 1' (30 cm) spaghetti length.

3. Turn to the page in *Strega Nona* where she is hanging up a "help wanted" sign. Ask the children what they think it said and then have them complete Help Wanted (page 8).

4. Take your children on a field trip to a local grocery store to discover the many shapes and varieties of pasta and pasta sauces. If going to the grocery store is not possible, save the food ad sections from your local newspapers and have the children explore the pasta shapes and varieties of sauces described in the ads.

5. Have the children create Big Anthony's overflowing pasta pot by making the flip book (reproduced on white construction paper) found on pages 9 and 10.

Overview of Activities

Extending the Book

1. Put your children into groups of three. For each group, tape a long piece of white adding-machine paper to a wall area (the hallway works well for this activity). Have the children draw mini-scenes from the story *Strega Nona* in sequential order. When they are done, have each team share their mini-sequenced story with the rest of the children.

2. With your children, look back in the story *Strega Nona* to the page that contains Strega Nona's pasta pot poem. Provide the children with copies of Strega Nona's pasta pot and yellow yarn noodles (page 11). Following the directions on page 11, have the children assemble their pasta pots. Encourage them to memorize Strega Nona's poem.

3. Suppose Big Anthony had blown three kisses instead of two. What would have happened to Big Anthony and the town? As a large group, or as an individual writing activity, have the children write a new ending wherein Big Anthony does blow three kisses. For an additional writing experience, discuss how the story might have been different if Big Anthony had followed Strega Nona's directions and had not touched her pasta pot. What other mischief might he have gotten into? Brainstorm some ideas. Then have the children write new tales of Big Anthony's adventures.

4. Share the background "history" of both Strega Nona and Big Anthony by reading their own stories, *Big Anthony: His Story*, and *Strega Nona: Her Story,* both by Tomie dePaola (Bibliography, page 79).

5. Artistically create plates of pretend pasta (page 56). Then fix an edible pasta treat using your favorite spaghetti recipe or a pre-packaged version.

6. Ask the children to think about what their family most often adds to plain pasta (such as tomato sauce, oil, basil leaves, etc.). Have the children write a story about a family pasta meal experience (real or make-believe).

7. Enjoy reading and/or memorizing the poem Family Favorite (page 29).

8. Print the letters S-P-A-G-H-E-T-T-I on the chalkboard. Challenge your children to make as many small words as possible from that large word within a specific amount of time.

Help Wanted

Strega Nona posted a sign to try to get someone to help around her house. What did the sign say?

HELP WANTED

_____

_____

_____

_____

_____

_____

Contact Strega Nona

Big Anthony's Pasta Pot

Cut out the 16 mini-pages. Staple them in order from 1 (the top page) to 16 (the bottom page) along the *left* side edge. Flip the pages from front to back and watch the pasta pot overflow!

Big Anthony's Pasta Pot *(cont.)*

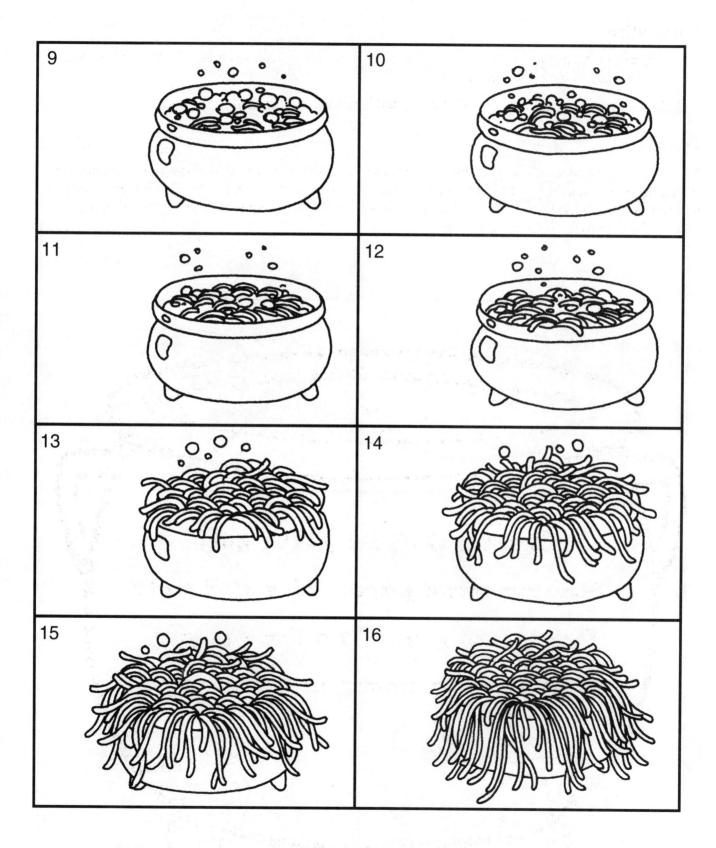

Strega Nona's Pasta Pot

Preparation

1. Reproduce the pasta pot below onto gray construction paper, one per child. Cut the slit line *only* with a sharp knife point or razor blade.

2. Cut yellow yarn into 8" (20 cm) lengths. Each child will need 10 lengths.

Directions

Have the children cut out their pasta pots. Then have them "even up" one end of their yarn lengths and thread the ends through the cut slit from the *backside* of the pot until 2" (5 cm) of the yarn lengths are still behind the pot. Provide each child with a strip of masking or transparent tape to tape down the ends of the yarn to the backside of the pot.

slit

Bubble, bubble pasta pot,

Boil me some pasta, nice and hot,

I'm hungry and it's time to sup,

Boil enough pasta to fill me up!

Pasta

by Kate Haycock

Summary

This informative book explains how pasta is made and enjoyed by people throughout the world. Pasta also describes the history and nutritional value of this popular food, as well as describing pasta shapes and the process of making pasta from the factory to store shelves. Recipes and illustrations are included for making fresh pasta and preparing a variety of pasta dishes.

The outline below is a suggested plan for using the various activities that are presented in this unit.

Sample Plan

Lesson I

- Explore pasta (page 13, Setting the Stage, #1).
- Read the Eating Pasta poem as a large group (page 29).
- Read *Pasta.*
- Assemble Pasta Pictionaries (page 13, Enjoying the Book, #1).
- Learn the names of pasta from around the world (page 13, Enjoying the Book, #2).

Lesson II

- Review *Pasta* and the Pasta Pictionary names and pronunciations.
- Learn the steps for Making Fresh Pasta (page 18).
- Start Cooking up Pasta Facts (page 19).
- Make Greek Orzo Salad or another pasta dish (pages 60–61).
- Create pasta graphs using Shapes Galore! (page 38).

Lesson III

- Learn about the history of pasta by completing the Pasta History Time Line (page 52).
- Complete From Factory to Store (page 14).
- Create original pasta sentences (page 13, Enjoying the Book, #5).
- Design Pasta Collages (page 57).
- Conduct Pasta Relay Races (page 62).
- Conduct one of the Writing Ideas (pages 31–32).

Lesson IV

- Review *Pasta* and focus on the fact that many pasta sauces contain tomatoes. Complete one or all of the tomato activities: Incredible Edible Tomatoes (page 44); A Tomato Plant (page 45); Tomato Sauce (page 46).
- Conduct the Truth in Advertising experiment (page 49).
- Can You Say it Better (page 34)?

Overview of Activities

Setting the Stage

1. Give each child a piece of shaped dry pasta. Ask the children to describe how it looks, feels, and smells. If the children want to, allow them to taste the dry pasta. Share that pasta has a better smell and taste when it is boiled in water for a few minutes. If possible, boil water and allow the children to taste the cooked pasta.

2. Show the visual process of making pasta from "field to packaging" on pages 12 and 13 of *Pasta*. Then complete the activity From Factory to Store (page 14).

Enjoying the Book

1. Have the children assemble individual Italian Pasta Pictionaries (page 16). Practice pronouncing the names of the different pasta shapes:

   angel hair (Ain-jel hare)   cannelloni (kan-eh-Loh-nee)
   fusilli (fyoo-See-lee)   lasagne (luh-Zahn-yuh)
   linguine (lihn-Gwee-nee)   macaroni (mak-uh-Roh-nee)
   penne (Pen-nay)   ravioli (rav-ee-Oh-lee)
   spaghetti (spuh-Geht-ee)   tortellini (tohr-tl-Eee-nee)
   vermicelli (ver-mih-Chehl-ee)

2. Have the children learn more about the names of pasta meals around the world. Provide each child with a copy of page 15 and work through it together. (Answers and pronunciations are located in the Answer Key, page 80.)

3. Conduct one or more of the suggested pasta math activities (page 38).

4. Complete Making Fresh Pasta (page 18) as a large group, or have the children work in small groups or with a partner.

5. Have children dictate original sentences about pasta. Write the sentences on sentence strips. Have the children cut up their own sentences into individual word cards (be certain the children label the back of each cut word with their initials or other identifiable mark so the sentences, if mixed up, can easily be resorted). After cutting into word cards, have each child mix up his or her own sentence and put it back in correct sequential word order. As an extension, place children into groups of two or three. Have them mix up all of their words and then sort out their original sentences. Next have them mix up their sentence words again and see if they can make up new sentences using the combined word cards.

Extending the Book

1. Make a copy of Cooking up Pasta Facts (page 19) for each child. Read through the sheet together, then have the children select three questions they would like to answer individually or in small groups. If possible, have cookbooks available for the children to complete this activity. If cookbooks are not available, make the activity a homework assignment.

2. Get some exercise indoors or outdoors by conducting a Pasta Relay Race (page 62).

From Factory to Store

Cut and paste the pictures in correct order, using a new piece of paper or a sentence strip.

Pasta Around the World

Match each country to its famous pasta meal by writing the pasta name next to the correct country.

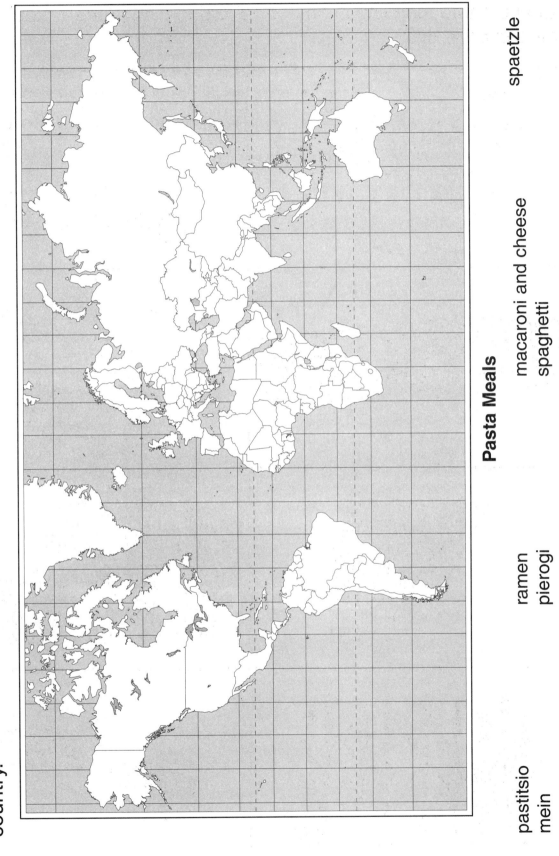

Pasta Meals

spaetzle

macaroni and cheese
spaghetti

ramen
pierogi

pastitsio
mein

Italian Pasta Pictionary

Cut apart the mini-pages and stack them in ABC order. Staple the pages on the *left* side edge to make a book.

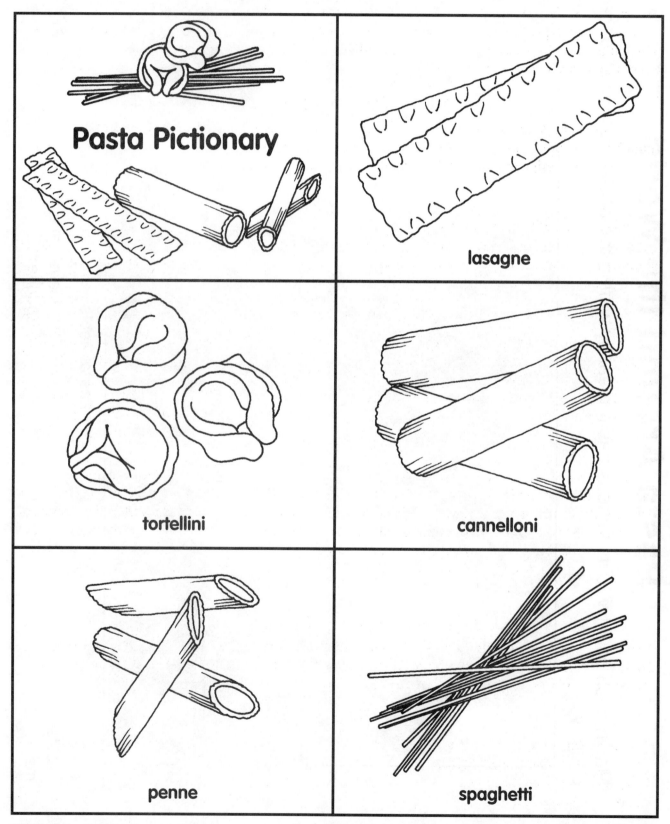

Italian Pasta Pictionary *(cont.)*

macaroni

fusilli

linguine

vermicelli

ravioli

angel hair

Making Fresh Pasta

In the boxes below, draw the things you need to make fresh pasta.

flour	egg	fork
rolling pin	knife	pasta pot

Read and number the sentences in the correct order (1–10).

_____ Use a fork to mix together the flour and egg.

_____ Use your hands to knead the pasta dough.

_____ Measure one cup of flour onto a flat surface.

_____ Break one egg into the flour.

_____ Roll the dough out very thin.

_____ Make a well in the cup of flour.

_____ Let the dough rest for 15 minutes.

_____ Cook the pasta in boiling water for 1–2 minutes.

_____ Bring a pot of water to boil.

_____ Cut the dough into the shapes you want.

Cooking up Pasta Facts

America

The dish **macaroni and cheese** was brought to America by settlers from England, but the most popular pasta dishes were brought to America from Italy. Over the years,  Italian people moved to America and opened grocery stores and restaurants. They shared their favorite **spaghetti** and **lasagne** dishes.

Asia

People in Asian countries eat many different kinds of noodles. The noodles are made from rice, buckwheat, or mung bean starch. Asian noodles are eaten plain, fried, cold, or in soups. Egg noodles are called **mein** in China, **ramen** in Japan, and **ba mee** in Thailand.

Europe

Pasta dough is used to make noodles and dumplings in Europe. Germans enjoy **spaetzle**, rich egg dumplings, served in stews or with gravies and sauces. Polish **pierogi** is pasta stuffed with cabbage or meat fillings.

Choose three of the following questions to answer. Use cookbooks to help you find your answers. Include the page numbers where you found your answers.

1. What are the names of five different Asian noodle dishes?
2. What ingredients are in the Greek dish *pastitsio*?
3. How is *spaetzle* cooked?
4. What foods can be stuffed inside *ravioli*?
5. What are *wonton*? How are they prepared?
6. What ingredients are in *gnocchi*?
7. What are the Italian names for these pasta shapes: string, tube, and ribbon?

Pizza Fit for a Queen

by Cynthia Holzschuher

Summary

This mini-book tells the account of the true story of how a popular Italian-style pizza was created. The rhyming text makes the story fun to read, and the Pizza Margherita recipe bakes up to be a fun treat to eat!

The outline below is a suggested plan for using the various activities presented in this unit.

Sample Plan

Lesson I

- Have the children assemble and read the *Pizza Fit for a Queen* mini-books (page 21, Setting the Stage, #1).
- Prepare and bake Pizza Margherita (recipe, page 26).
- After taste-testing Pizza Margherita, complete the Restaurant Review (page 27).
- Recite the Pizza Pie poem (page 29).
- Complete the Pizza Fractions activity (page 39).
- Choose one of the Writing Ideas (pages 31–32).

Lesson II

- Read a big book version of *Pizza Fit for a Queen* (page 21, Enjoying the Book, #1), focusing on rhyming words as well as reviewing the story content.
- Remind the children that the story *Pizza Fit for a Queen* took place in Naples, Italy. Locate Naples on your Italy bulletin-board display (page 70). Complete A Naples Pizzeria (page 37).
- Design Pizza Creations (page 28).
- Discover A World of Toppings (page 50).
- Conduct the Pizza Dough "Kneads" Yeast science experiment (page 48).

Lesson III

- Learn The Story of Pizza Hut (page 51).
- Create Pizza History Time Lines (page 53).

- Create a Pizza Pie Story (page 39).
- Conduct the Chopped-Up Vegetable Volume experiment (page 39).
- Decide if the toppings are More or Less (page 42).
- Complete Pizza Cut-Ups (page 40).
- Explore senses with Poetry Makes Sense (page 30).

Lesson IV

- Have a Pasta and Pizza Day. Start by reviewing the Pasta and Pizza History Time Lines (page 52 and 53).
- Create Pasta and Pizza Songs (page 58).
- Create Pasta and Pizza Menu story problems (page 41).
- Describe it, Please! (page 35).
- Explore the verb ending *-ed* (page 36).
- Create Pasta and Pizza Plates (page 56).

Lesson V

- Review the *Pizza Fit for a Queen* story via created mini-books or big book.
- Share the culminating activity concepts (page 64).
- Begin to plan the Operetta Extravaganza! (page 65).
- Play the Pizza Game (page 73).

Overview of Activities

Setting the Stage

1. Have each child color, cut out, and assemble a mini-book version of *Pizza Fit for a Queen*. Read the story as a total group, or meet with the children in smaller reading groups. Focus on the concept of the story itself, as well as reinforcing language skills, such as identifying the rhyming words.

Enjoying the Book

1. Create a big book version of *Pizza Fit for a Queen* (pages 22–26). The enlarging process can be completed using a copying machine with enlarging features or by making overhead transparencies of the mini-pages using an overhead projector to project the book pages onto bulletin-board or chart paper and tracing the illustrations and text.

2. Collect pizza menus from local restaurants and have the children role-play ordering pizzas. Encourage them to make price comparisons as they order (for example, the price of pizza usually goes up quickly when extra toppings are added).

3. Reproduce the Pizza Slice writing page (page 33), one page per child. On the "inside" portion of the pizza slice, have each child write about his or her favorite kind of pizza. On the front cover of the pizza slice, have each child draw an illustration of his or her favorite pizza topping(s).

4. Complete some or all of the math pizza activities (page 39).

5. Read the poem (more of a chant) Three Cheers for PIZZA (page 29). After a few practice readings, try to have the children say the poem in a round. Finish up the activity by making quick pizzas (page 59).

Extending the Book

1. Complete the Nutritional Facts sheet (page 47).

2. Get in contact with the Pizza Hut *Book It!* Reading Incentive Program (Bibliography, page 79) which encourages your children to be active readers. The five-month program (October-February) is designed to allow children, kindergarten through sixth grade, to read at individually-assessed rates, and, by meeting stated monthly goals, receive a personal pan pizza certificate redeemable at any Pizza Hut restaurant. Each child is also awarded a *Book It!* wearable pin, monthly star sticker awards to be added to the pin, and an All-Star Reading Medallion, awarded only if a child reaches all five months of his or her predetermined reading goals.

3. Begin the process of planning the unit's culminating activities which includes performing an operetta based on the story *Pizza Fit for a Queen*. Pages 64 and 65 will help you prepare for this special event.

4. Compare the similarities and differences of pasta and pizza by creating a Venn diagram.

Pizza Fit for a Queen

Pizza Fit for a Queen

This book belongs to _____

My name is Rafaele Esposito. I'm from Naples, Italy.

I make pasta and pizza in my shop—both plain and fancy.

1

Pizza Fit for a Queen *(cont.)*

One day my friend, Marcello, came to my kitchen door.

"The queen is coming to Naples," he said, "Your pizza she does adore!"

2

I wonder what I can do to honor Queen Margherita?

Would she like spaghetti, ravioli, or maybe . . . a pizza?

3

Pizza Fit for a Queen (cont.)

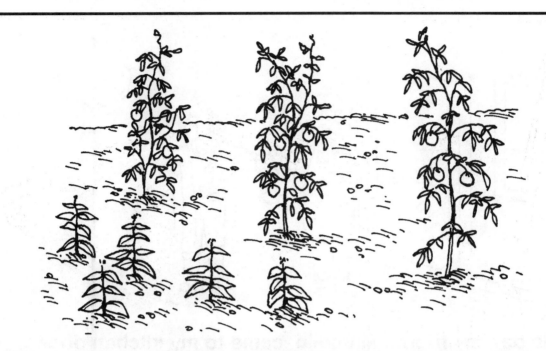

I went out to my garden, and what did I see?

Red tomatoes and green basil leaves staring back at me.

4

CHEESE

I then got an idea that was sure to please.

I ran to the market to get some white cheese!

5

Pizza Fit for a Queen *(cont.)*

I'll make my pizza look like the flag of Italy!

I'll call it Pizza Margherita in honor of her royalty.

6

The queen tasted my pizza and raised up her hand.

She proclaimed it was the best pizza in all the land!

7

Pizza Fit for a Queen *(cont.)*

Pizza Margherita was created in the year 1889.

To this day it is a pizza many find divine!

8

Pizza Margherita

2 tubes refrigerated pizza dough
8 ounces (225 g) basil leaves
1 pound (450 g) grated mozzarella cheese
2–3 large tomatoes, sliced thin
garlic powder, oregano, salt, and pepper

1. Preheat the oven to 450° F (230° C).
2. Shape and spread the dough pieces into one flat rectangle on a baking sheet.
3. Arrange the basil leaves over the left third of the dough, the cheese over the middle third, and the tomato slices over the remaining right third.
4. Sprinkle the entire pizza with the garlic powder, oregano, salt, and pepper to taste.
5. Bake for 12–15 minutes or until the crust is golden brown. Remove the pizza from the oven. *Bon Apetito!*

9

Restaurant Review

You just ate Pizza Margherita at Rafaele's Pizzeria. Write a pizza review. Use as many adjectives as you can to describe the pizza. Give reasons to support your opinion of how the pizza tasted.

The Naples Restaurant Review

A New Pizza for Italy!

Read about the pizza fit for a queen at Rafaele's Pizzeria!

_____

_____

_____

_____

_____

_____

_____

_____

The Famous Pizza Margherita

_____

_____

_____

_____

_____

_____

Pizza Creations

Rafaele Esposito created a pizza for the queen that looked like the Italian flag. Now it's your turn to create a pizza for your family's dinner. Think about the toppings they would enjoy eating. Draw your family's pizza on the crust below. Label the foods you used on your pizza.

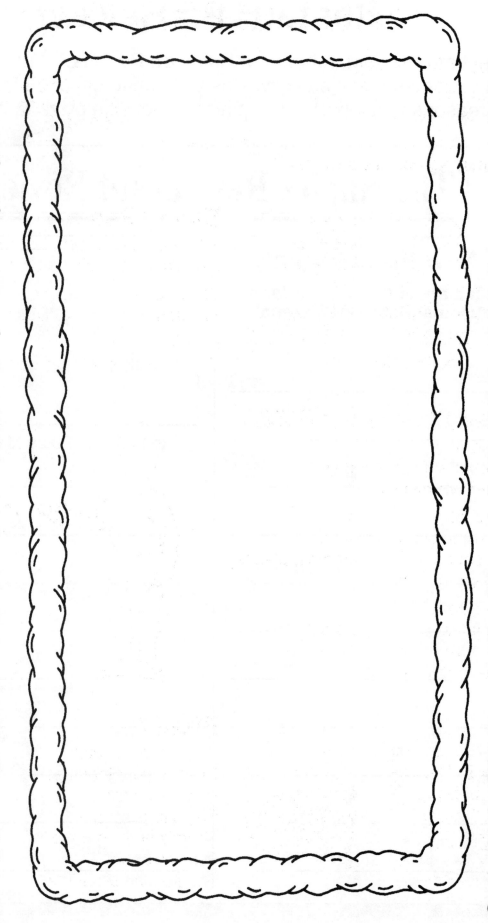

On the back of this paper, write why you chose the ingredients you did to create your family's pizza.

Pasta and Pizza Poems

Family Favorite

I'm always ready to eat spaghetti.
It's my favorite dinner.

With meatballs and cheese, it's sure to please.
My family agrees–it's a winner!

Eating Pasta

Ribbons, spirals, tubes, and strings,
Pasta's shaped like many things.

Boil in water, serve it hot.
Pile some meat and sauce on top.

I'm so hungry, I can hardly wait.
Eating pasta's really great!

Three Cheers for PIZZA

P-I-Z-Z-A!
We could eat it every day!
Pizza–*m-m-m*–pizza.

P-I-Z-Z-A!
Pepperoni, chewy cheese,
Extra sauce and mushrooms, please.
Pizza–*m-m-m*–pizza.

P-I-Z-Z-A!
Make it fast and serve it hot,
Pizza sure does hit the spot.
Pizza–*m-m-m*–pizza!

Pizza Pie

Pie, pie, pizza pie!
Choose your toppings,
Pile them high.
Pie, pie, pizza pie!
There's nothing better,
In any weather,
Than eating pizza pie!

Poetry Makes Sense

Read the senses poem.

Line 1 (taste)   **Mom's pizza is hot and spicy,**
Line 2 (sight)   **Covered with red sauce and green pepper, too.**
Line 3 (touch) **Pulled out of the oven, hot to the table,**
Line 4 (smell) **It smells so good it makes my stomach growl.**
Line 5 (feel)   **M-m-m, chewy crust makes my teeth work hard!**

Now it's your turn. Write a sense poem about your favorite pasta or pizza dish.

_____

Line 1 (taste)

_____

Line 2 (sight)

_____

Line 3 (touch)

_____

Line 4 (smell)

_____

Line 5 (feel)

Draw a picture of your favorite pasta or pizza dish.

Writing Ideas

Pocket Charts

If you do not have access to a pre-made pocket chart, you can easily make one for use in reading groups or at learning centers. Begin by laminating a 24" x 36" (61 cm x 91 cm) piece of brightly-colored tagboard. Run an additional 27" (69 cm) piece of lamination plastic through the laminator. (You will not be running tagboard through the machine this time; you will be running only the lamination plastic through the machine.) Cut the lamination plastic into nine equal strips (each strip will be 3"/8 cm depth-wise). You will be placing the cut strips onto the laminated tagboard backpiece to form the pocket chart's pockets.

To begin the pocket-forming process, lay one of the pocket strips near the top edge (24"/61 cm wide) of the laminated tagboard (the tagboard should be laying flat for easier handling). Tape down the sides and bottom of the pocket strip using transparent tape to form the first pocket. Lay down a second pocket strip directly under the just-taped pocket (make certain that the bottom of the taped pocket is just above the top of the newly-placed pocket strip). Tape as you did with the first strip. Continue this process until you have taped down all nine pockets. Reinforce the edges of the pocket chart by taping all four of the outside edges with a strip of the clear packaging tape. Your nine-pocket pocket chart is now ready to be stood upright on a chalkrail or easel. You can also punch holes near the top of the pocket chart and hang it for display.

Suggestions for using pocket charts include reading displayed poems (page 29), spelling and/or reading vocabulary words from the word bank (page 32), sequencing the pasta and pizza history time lines (pages 52 and 53), or sequencing pasta- and pizza-making steps. The following sentences sequence the steps for making a pizza.

1.	**Make the pizza dough and pizza sauce.**
2.	**Spread the pizza dough on a baking sheet.**
3.	**Pour the pizza sauce over the dough.**
4.	**Sprinkle some cheese on the pizza sauce.**
5.	**Add your favorite pizza toppings.**
6.	**Bake the pizza in a hot oven.**

Daily Journal Writing

Choose one of the questions or statements listed below and write it on a chalkboard or chart paper. Younger children may illustrate their responses while older children both write and illustrate their responses.

- *What do you like on your pizza? Pasta? Why?*
- *Which is better for dinner, pizza or spaghetti? Why?*
- *If you could create a dessert pizza, how would you make it?*
- *What kind of pizza or pasta meal would you create for the president of the United States?*
- *Try to write the recipe and directions for your family's favorite pasta dish.*
- *Pretend you are the owner of a new pizzeria. Write a menu.*
- *Create a tasty pizza that a dog or cat would enjoy eating.*

Writing Ideas *(cont.)*

Pasta or Pizza Prose

The word prose is defined as "ordinary language, not poetry." In other words, ordinary language becomes poetry when it rhymes or has a rhythm. Challenge your children to create pasta or pizza prose. For example:

Pizza is the Best!

I like pizza
and could eat it every day.
I have lots of favorite toppings.
The best one is pepperoni.

I like pizza
as a special Saturday treat.
That is when my family
spends special time together.

Pasta and Pizza Word Bank

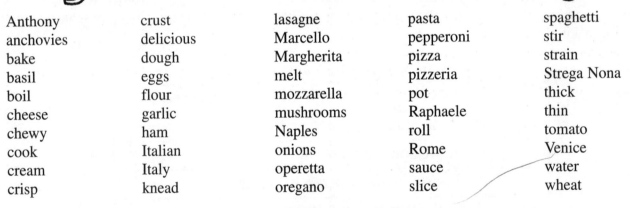

Anthony	crust	lasagne	pasta	spaghetti
anchovies	delicious	Marcello	pepperoni	stir
bake	dough	Margherita	pizza	strain
basil	eggs	melt	pizzeria	Strega Nona
boil	flour	mozzarella	pot	thick
cheese	garlic	mushrooms	Raphaele	thin
chewy	ham	Naples	roll	tomato
cook	Italian	onions	Rome	Venice
cream	Italy	operetta	sauce	water
crisp	knead	oregano	slice	wheat

A word bank is a wonderful resource for children to have available while writing creative stories, recipes, or poetry. You may want to post the word bank on a bulletin-board display, writing the words on paper pizza slices made out of cut bulletin-board paper, or have the children create personal pasta and pizza vocabulary dictionaries. Some other possible uses for the word bank words are . . .

—flashcards   —alphabetizing   —pocket chart practice

—crossword puzzles   —spelling lessons   —word search puzzles

Writing on a Piece-a Pizza

On the following page you will find a pizza slice pattern that can be used for individual creative writing time, copying pizza recipes, building definitions for pizza words generated from the word bank above, or may be used for creating invitations to invite guests to the Operetta Extravaganza! culminating activity (page 64).

Pizza Slice

See page 32 for directions.

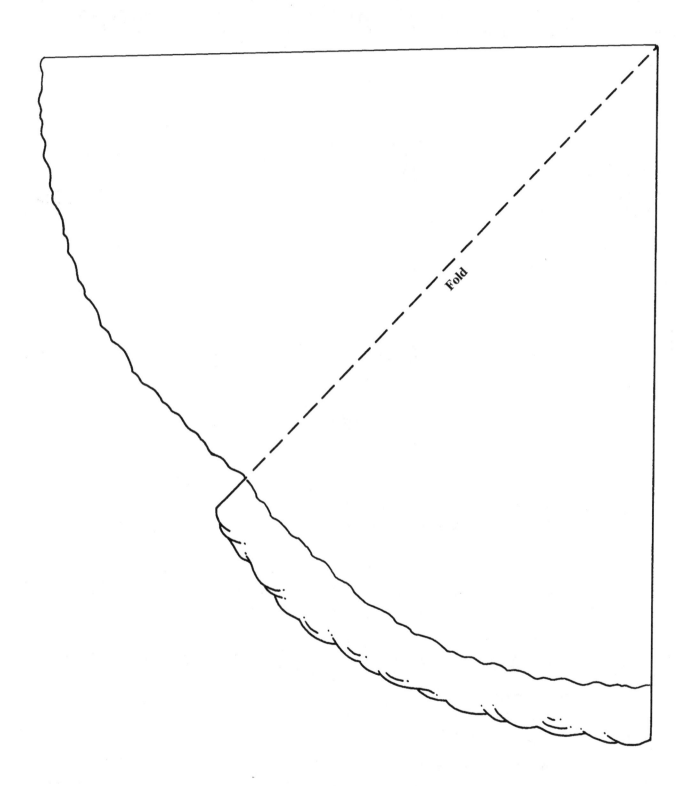

Fold

Can You Say it Better?

Transforming sentences involves changing words in a sentence while leaving the sentence's basic structure and context intact. This writing strategy introduces children to the process of creating more complex and interesting sentences. Look at the sample sentence transformation below. The italicized words or phrases in the original sentence were changed yet the transformed sentence makes sense and overall, still has the same meaning.

Original

Noodles *made* with *flour, water, and eggs* are used in *soups*.

Transformation

Noodles *created* with *rice flour* are used in *Chinese appetizers*.

Remember when conducting sentence transformation activities with your children:

1. Brainstorm an array of possible changes and record those possibilities on a chalkboard or chart paper.
2. Make up sentences that will also provide practice in specific language arts skills, such as capital letters, commas in a series, or punctuation marks.
3. Be certain of your children's level of ability. If the sample sentences below prove too difficult for your children, try using the suggestions in the Simple Sentences section.

Sample Sentences for Transformation

These sentences are adapted from *Pasta* (page 12). Write them on a large piece of chart paper or chalkboard area. Discuss possible transformations before having the children write their own versions.

1. *Italy* is one of the *places* where people *eat a lot of pasta*.
2. *Athletes* may eat a *large bowl of pasta* before a *race*.
3. Homemade *pasta* is not *difficult* to *make*.
4. You can buy *pasta* in many *shapes* and *colors*.
5. In *recent years*, *doctors* have encouraged people to *eat* more *pasta*.
6. Pasta is a *favorite* dish *served* around the *world*.

Simple Sentences

If the transformation sentences above are too difficult, create simpler sentences wherein the children change only one noun, one verb, or one adjective per sentence. For example:

Original	Transformation
Pasta is fun to eat.	*Spaghetti* is fun to eat.

When the children are comfortable with the transformation concept, have them change two words per sentence, such as a noun and a verb.

Original	Transformation
The pizza was *topped* with *meat*.	The pizza was *covered* with *pepperoni*.

Describe it, Please!

Adjectives describe people, places, or things.

I like to eat **hot, thick, chewy** pizza.

I like to eat **red, spicy, tomato** sauce on my pasta.

Write three adjectives to describe each food below.

_____, _____, _____ **crust**

_____, _____, _____ **spaghetti**

_____, _____, _____ **sauce**

_____, _____, _____ **cheese**

_____, _____, _____ **tomato**

Write a pasta or pizza story using as many adjectives (describing words) as you can.

Title: _____

_____

_____

_____

_____

_____

_____

_____

_____

_____

_____

Draw a picture about your story on the back of this paper.

Verbs

Verbs are words that show action.

Use the words in the verb box below to complete the sentences. You will need to add the *-ed* ending to each verb.

Pizza Time

Mother _____ the dough for five minutes and then _____ the dough flat. She added the toppings and _____ the pizza in the hot oven. The cheese _____. The pizza _____ so good! Mother took the pizza out of the oven and _____ the pizza into eight equal slices. She then _____ a salad to eat with the pizza.

Pasta Time

Mother _____ the garlic and added it to the sauce pot. The sauce had to be _____ so it would not burn. Dad _____ the freshly-made sauce. Mother _____ the dry pasta in boiling water. We then _____ eating our spaghetti and meatballs dinner.

Verb Box

taste	enjoy	stir	melt
knead	roll	smell	cook
chop	divide	prepare	bake

A Naples Pizzeria

Read the following story carefully. Can you find all of the mistakes?
Proofread the story.

Circle punctuation mistakes. What time is it⦰

Underline capitalization mistakes. Mr. s̲mith is angry.

Cross out spelling mistakes and spell them correctly. ba̶k̶ker *baker*

Pizzaiolos

Piza from Naples is famous, and so are the town's pizza bakers. In Napels, italy, a pizzaiolo must follow special rules when making pizzas. The pizzaiolo prepares his ingredients fresh every day   The dough must contain only flour, water, yeast, and salt? It must be kneeded by hand and baked in a wood-burning brick oven at 750 degrees F   The spices and tomatos used must have been grown in the soil of the nearby volcano, mount vesuvius, and the mozzarella cheeze must be soft and frech? neopolitan pizza is said to bee the best pizza in all the world!

How many mistakes were in the story?

punctuation_____   capitalization_____   spelling _____

Based on the context clues, what do these words mean?

1. pizzaiolo _____

2. kneaded_____

3. Mt. Vesuvius _____

4. Neapolitan _____

Pasta-bilities

Colored Pasta

Materials (per color)

- ½ cup (120 mL) rubbing alcohol
- 8 ounces (225 g) dry pasta
- bowl
- paper towels
- food coloring, various colors
- 1 quart (1 liter) jar with lid
- strainer

Directions

1. Put the rubbing alcohol and the desired amount of food coloring into the quart (liter) jar. Place the lid on the jar, seal lid tightly, and shake the jar well.

2. Open the lid and add the dry pasta. Tighten the lid again and shake the jar until the pasta reaches the desired color. *Optional:* Allow the pasta to sit in the jar for awhile to deepen the color.

3. Place the strainer over the bowl and drain the pasta by pouring out the colored alcohol; discard the used alcohol. Lay the colored pasta out evenly onto a layer of paper towels. The pasta will be dry in approximately 15 minutes.

4. Repeat steps one through three using fresh rubbing alcohol for each color desired.

Shapes Galore!

Provide each child, or small group of children (do not exceed three per group), with one cup (225 g) of a mixed assortment of colored (see above) dry pasta noodles (such as wheel, tube, macaroni, spiral, and shell). Have the children sort the pasta by shape. Then have them count the total number of each shape and transfer the gained information to a 1" (2.54 cm) grid sheet (pasta graph) by coloring in the appropriate number of squares per colored pasta shape. Have the children determine which pasta shape they had the most of and the least of. For an extension, have the children glue their pasta shapes onto their pasta bar graphs.

Pasta Patterns

Using sentence strips, provide the children with an assortment of dried colored pasta shapes (see directions above) and have them create patterns by gluing down a repetitive sequence of pasta shells onto the sentence strips. Encourage the children to create a core pattern (the initial pattern) and extend the core pattern two times.

Practicing with Pizza

Pizza Fractions

Provide each child with crayons or markers and a 12" (30 cm)-diameter circle that has been cut out of light brown bulletin-board paper. Dictate fractional directions according to the abilities of your children. For example, "Draw sauce on one-half of your pizza," "Draw mushrooms on one-quarter of your pizza," or "Draw pepperoni on one-third and ham on two-thirds of your pizza."

Pizza Pie Story

In the fashion of *The Doorbell Rang*, by Pat Hutchins (Mulberry, 1989), have your children create a story based on two children who are ready to eat a pizza pie their mother baked (or that was just delivered from a pizza restaurant) that has been divided into sixteen slices. As the children are just about to eat their pizza, the doorbell rings . . .

After your children have created the pizza pie story outline (if you have a copy of *The Doorbell Rang*, you may want to review it or reread it to your children), have them write, edit, and revise the pizza pie story's text. Then create a big book version of the story and have the children illustrate their story's text.

To create the big book, use large sheets of paper (at least 12" x 18"/30 cm x 46 cm). The first sheet will be the book's cover. On the remaining sheets (pages), the children will illustrate the pages' text. After the illustrations are complete, stack the completed sheets in correct sequence (title page followed by each story page), align the edges, and staple the pages together along the left side edge to create the book's spine.

Chopped-Up Vegetable Volume

Display a variety of fresh vegetables that can be chopped up to top a pizza. (Suggested vegetables include tomatoes, green peppers, mushrooms, and onions.) Have the children study the shapes and sizes of the vegetables carefully. Show them a one-cup (225 g) measuring container. Ask them to predict how many of each type of vegetable will need to be chopped to equal one cup (225 g). Demonstrate the concept of "chopped up" by cutting one of the mushrooms. After the children have made their predictions, begin to chop up the vegetables and discover the results. (**Note:** It is highly recommended that you, or another adult, conduct all of the cutting of the vegetables).

Create a graph showing the results of how many of each vegetable had to be chopped up to equal one cup (225 g). Then, as a perfect closure to this activity, make Quick Pizzas (page 59) and top them with the chopped-up vegetables before baking.

Pizza Cut-Ups

Draw on 1/4 of the pizza.

Draw on 1/3 of the pizza.

Draw on 3/4 of the pizza.

Draw on 2/3 of the pizza.

Draw on 1/2 of the pizza.

Draw on 2/3 of the pizza.

Pasta and Pizza Menu

Use the menu to write two story problems and then give your paper to someone to try to solve your story problems.

Small cheese pizza $3.00	**—additional toppings $.50**
Medium cheese pizza $4.00	**—additional toppings $.75**
Large cheese pizza $6.00	**—additional toppings $1.00**
Spaghetti with tomato sauce $3.00	**—meatballs $1.00 each**
Lasagne $4.25	**Salad bar $2.50**
Meatball sandwich $3.50	**Soft drinks $.75**

Problem 1:   Work Area

_____

_____

_____

_____

_____

Problem 2:

_____

_____

_____

_____

_____

More or Less

Color, cut out, and paste the pictures in the correct boxes. Answer the question below each box.

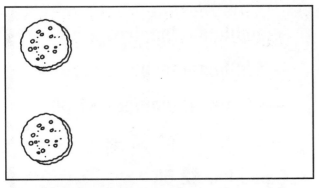

Are there *more* or *less* than 10 pepperoni?_____

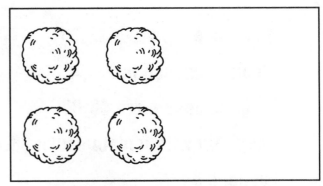

Are there *more* or *less* than 10 meatballs?_____

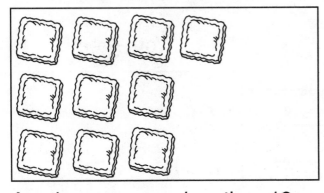

Are there *more* or *less* than 10 ravioli?_____

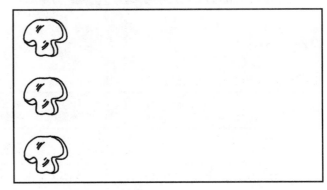

Are there *more* or *less* than 10 mushrooms?_____

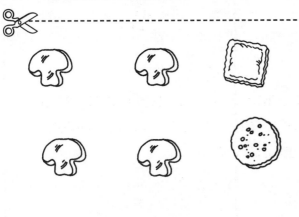

Is it Time to Eat?

Answer the questions by drawing hands on the clock faces to show the correct times.

1. At 4:30 p.m., Mom mixed the pasta dough. It took 30 minutes to mix, cook, drain, and serve the pasta. What time did we eat dinner?

Show the time on the clock.

2. By 5:00 p.m., Dad had made spaghetti with red sauce. He put it in a dish, topped it with cheese, and put the dish in the oven to bake for 30 minutes. What time did we eat dinner?

Show the time on the clock.

3. Our family had lasagne for dinner. Mom put the lasagne noodles in a pot of boiling water at 4:00 p.m. They needed to cook for 10 minutes. What time were the noodles ready?

Show the time on the clock.

4. It took 20 minutes to prepare the ravioli with sauce, meat, and cheese. Dad started preparing our dinner at 4:10 p.m. What time did he put the ravioli in the oven to bake?

Show the time on the clock.

Incredible Edible Tomatoes

The tomato, originally from South America, was first brought to Europe in the early 1500s. In those days, tomatoes were thought to be poisonous, so many people were afraid to eat them. Soon people learned that they were not only safe to eat but tasty as well. The first cookbook to contain tomato recipes was published in Naples, Italy, in 1692. By the 1800s tomatoes had become popular in England and the United States.

Americans eat more tomatoes each year than any other vegetable or fruit, except potatoes. Tomatoes consist of mostly water and contain no fat or cholesterol. They are a good source of vitamin A, vitamin C, and potassium.

There are six main parts to a tomato plant: the roots, the stem, the leaves, the vine, the blossoms, and the fruit. There are many varieties of tomatoes, such as cherry, plum, and giant red. You can find out more information about this wonderful vegetable by visiting the Web site: www.tomato.com.

Choose one or all of the activities suggested below to complete as a large group, small group, or individual projects.

Activities

1. Research a list of vegetables in the nightshade (any flowering plant related to the potato or tomato) family. Try to find out the name of the one plant from the nightshade family that is poisonous.

2. Learn how vitamin A, vitamin C, and potassium help the human body.

3. Display tomatoes from the red, yellow, orange, and green varieties. Have the children taste each one and compare flavors and textures.

4. Collect your children's favorite family recipes that use tomatoes as an ingredient. Reproduce the recipes and bind them into a class cookbook.

5. Brainstorm a list of processed tomato products (such as SpagettiOs® or salsa).

6. Invent a new processed food that has tomatoes as a main ingredient. Give the new food a name. If desired, have your children design a "marketing plan" including a slogan, packaging look, and one form of advertisement.

7. Plant tomato seeds, or start with seedlings, and watch them grow!

A Tomato Plant

Label the tomato plant.

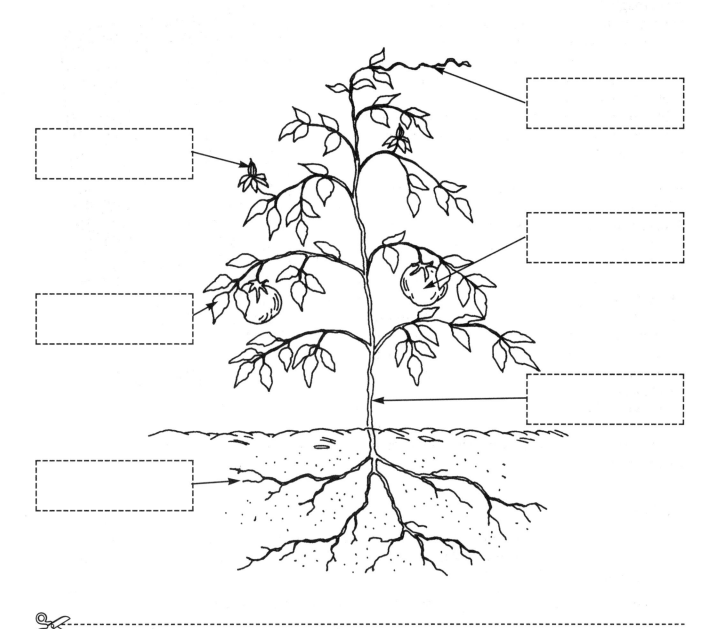

✂ ---

Cut and paste.

roots	**stem**	**leaves**
vine	**fruit**	**blossom**

Tomato Sauce

Cut and paste the pictures in order on a sentence strip to tell the story of tomatoes from plant to sauce.

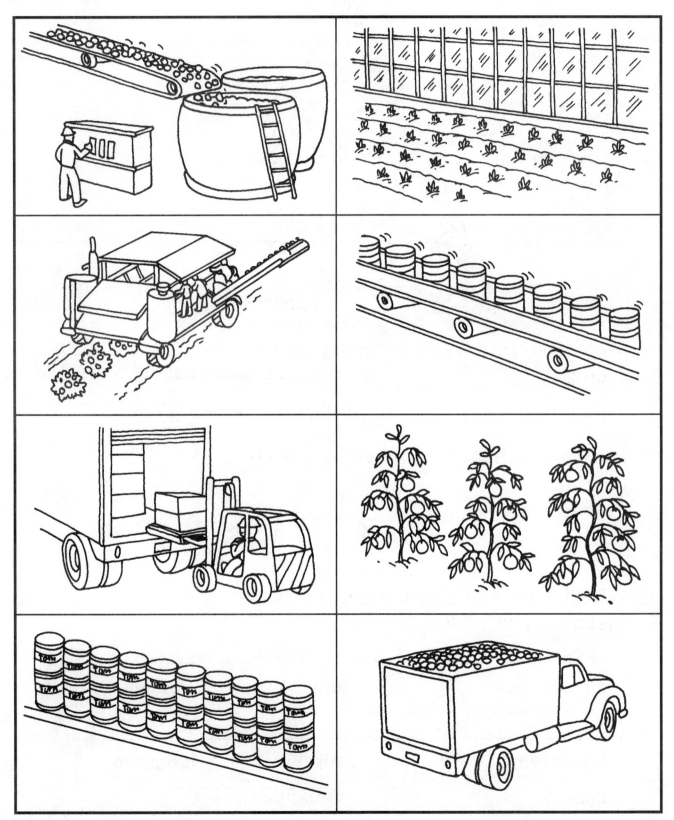

Nutritional Facts

Study the food pyramid and answer the four questions below.

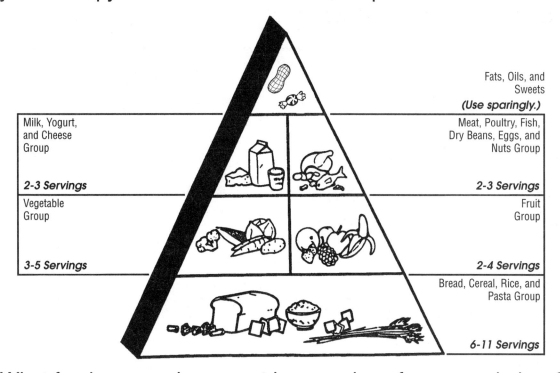

1. What food groups do you eat in a serving of pepperoni pizza?

   crust _____   tomato sauce_____

   pepperoni_____   cheese_____

2. What food groups do you eat in a serving of macaroni and cheese?

   macaroni _____   cheese_____

   butter _____   milk _____

3. What food groups do you eat in a serving of spaghetti and meatballs topped with cheese?

   spaghetti _____   meatballs_____

   cheese _____   tomato sauce_____

4. What food groups do you eat in a serving of eggplant lasagne?

   lasagne _____   eggplant_____

   cheese _____   tomato sauce_____

Pizza Dough "Kneads" Yeast

Pizza dough is made from flour, water, sugar, and yeast. Yeast is a fungus that makes dough expand or rise. It feeds on sugar, then releases carbon dioxide gas which gets trapped in the dough. Yeast dough must be kneaded to help the ingredients mix and to create gluten. Gluten is an elastic substance in flour that gives dough its sturdy structure. After kneading, the dough must "rest" in a warm place. This allows the yeast to eat the sugar and make the carbon dioxide gas.

In this experiment, the children will visually experience the rising action of yeast as well as taste-test baked yeast dough versus baked no-yeast dough.

Materials

- 4 cups (900 g) flour
- 1 teaspoon (5 mL) sugar
- 1½ cups (360 mL) warm water
- 1 teaspoon (5 mL) salt
- 2 tablespoons (30 mL) olive oil
- 2 teaspoons (10 mL) active dry yeast

Utensils

- 2 large bowls
- 2 small towels
- 1 small bowl
- 2 pizza pie pans
- 1 wooden spoon

1. In each bowl, place 2 cups (450 g) flour, ½ teaspoon (2.5 mL) salt, ½ teaspoon (2.5 mL) sugar, and 1 tablespoon (15 mL) olive oil; mix well with the wooden spoon.

2. Add ¾ cup (180 mL) water to the contents of one bowl only; mix well with the wooden spoon. Hand-knead the dough for about five minutes on a flat surface to make a soft dough. Place the dough back into the bowl; cover with a towel and set aside.

3. In the small bowl, combine ¾ cup (180 mL) warm water (100° F/45° C) with the 2 teaspoons (10 mL) dry yeast; set aside and allow to sit for five minutes.

4. Make a hole in the center of the flour mixture in the second large bowl and add the yeast mixture to it. Mix well and knead for about five minutes on a flat surface. (If the dough is too sticky, add a little extra flour.) Form the dough into a smooth ball, place it back into its bowl, and cover the bowl with a towel. Allow the dough to rise for about one hour in a warm dark place.

5. Remove the small towels from both bowls of dough. Have the children observe the two doughs and make comparisons. Discuss the effect the yeast had on the second batch of dough.

6. Flatten both dough batches and place them on the two pizza pans. (Do not mix up the doughs. Be certain you know which one contains the yeast, and which one doesn't.) Add desired pizza toppings and bake for 20 minutes at 400° F (200° C). Remove the pizzas from the oven; cool slightly. Divide the pizzas so that all the children get a small tasting sample of both baked pizza doughs. Which dough do they think tastes the best? Why?

Using Your Head

In this experiment, your children will use their senses to identify the smell and taste of garlic, oregano, and basil.

Materials

- crackers
- fresh oregano
- butter
- fresh garlic
- fresh basil

Utensils

- cutting board
- plastic knives
- blindfolds
- writing paper
- pencils
- chopping knife (to be used by an adult only)

Directions

1. If possible, show the children photos of garlic, basil, and oregano plants in a well-illustrated cookbook. Explain that herbs (pronounced "urbs") are plants used for medicines or for seasoning foods.

2. Display the herb leaves and garlic bulbs. Dice the herbs on the cutting board with the chopping knife. (**Note:** Be certain to clean the knife after each herb is diced so that the flavors are not being accidentally mixed.) Allow the children to smell each individual diced herb.

3. Have the children, or helping adults, sprinkle a little bit of each herb onto lightly-buttered crackers (each child will be getting a total of three herbed crackers: garlic, oregano, and basil).

4. Provide a blindfold for every two children. One child is blindfolded while his or her partner provides the three types of herb-prepared crackers for the taste-testing experience. (**Important:** Make certain the children can identify the different types of herbs.) Upon tasting each herb cracker the blindfolded child tells the partner if he or she likes the taste. The partner records his or her response. When the child has sampled all three herbs, the blindfold is removed and the results shared. Then the children reverse roles.

5. When all the children have completed the taste-testing experience, gather them together and draw some conclusions about the tasted herbs based on the results.

Truth in Advertising

In this experiment, the children will compare the amount of water versus solids in two commercially-prepared pasta sauces.

Materials

- 2 one-cup (240 mL) measuring cups
- 2 brands of commercially-prepared spaghetti sauces
- 1 large spoon
- 2 medium-size bowls
- 2 strainers (must be able to fit over the rims of the bowls)

Directions

Place one strainer over each bowl. Measure one cup (240 mL) of each type of spaghetti sauce into the two measuring cups. Slowly pour the spaghetti sauces into the two strainer-covered bowls. Allow the sauces to drip through the strainers. When both sauces have completely separated (liquids in the bowls versus solids on top of the strainers), measure the liquid and solid portions individually using the measuring cups.

A World of Toppings

Pepperoni is the number one pizza topping in the United States, but people around the world like other foods on top of their pizzas. In England, pizzas are topped with tuna and corn, while Russians enjoy pizza topped with salmon and onions. In Brazil pizzas are topped with green peas. Barbecued chicken is a favorite topping with people in the Bahamas. Australians choose to top their pizzas with eggs. Pizzerias in Singapore flavor their beef and chicken toppings with chili flakes or curry powder. In India pizzas are topped with pickled ginger.

Draw a line to match the countries to their pizza toppings.

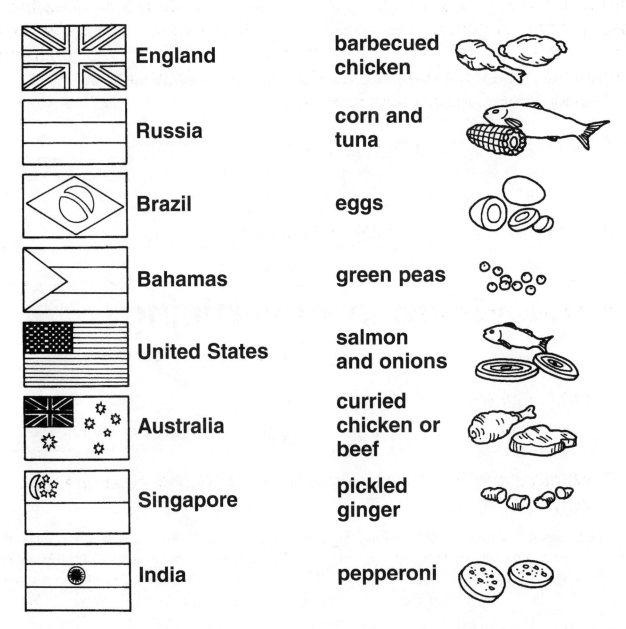

England

Russia

Brazil

Bahamas

United States

Australia

Singapore

India

barbecued chicken

corn and tuna

eggs

green peas

salmon and onions

curried chicken or beef

pickled ginger

pepperoni

The Story of Pizza Hut

Pizza Hut opened its doors in 1958. It was started by two brothers, Dan and Frank Carney, in Wichita, Kansas. Their mother lent them $600 to buy some used kitchen equipment and rent a small store. The brothers began by selling thin crust pizzas and drinks. Dan and Frank wanted Pizza Hut to offer its customers a quality

product, friendly service, and good value. They wanted to serve the best pizza in America. Dan and Frank added salads and sandwiches to the menu in 1970. In 1977 Pizza Hut was sold to a large restaurant organization called Tricon Global Restaurants. They also own Kentucky Fried Chicken and Taco Bell.

1. Who created Pizza Hut? When?

    _____

2. Where was the first restaurant located?

    _____

3. What did the first Pizza Hut serve?

    _____ and _____

4. What was added in 1970?

    _____ and _____

5. What other famous restaurants do Tricon Global Restaurants own?

    _____ and _____

Pasta History Time Line

Cut apart the fact cards and create a time line by gluing the cards in order on sentence strips or adding machine paper.

Three hundred years ago the English discovered pasta while exploring Italy and brought it to the New World. Thomas Jefferson, our third president, brought an Italian pasta machine to America. He used it to make spaghetti and lasagne noodles for his friends.

Thousands of years ago people in China made dough from flour and water. They found that it could be dried and later cooked in boiling water.

Today most dry pasta is produced in modern factories. Pasta shapes are made by pressing the dough into molds and then dried.

Five hundred years ago people in Italy were enjoying *macheroni*, the name given to pasta of all shapes. Each shape has its own special name, too.

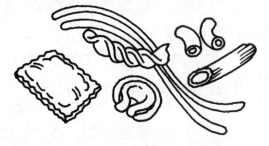

In 1295, Marco Polo, a young Italian explorer, visited the Middle East. Some people believe he brought pasta to Italy.

Pizza History Time Line

Cut apart the fact cards and create a time line by gluing the cards in order on sentence strips or adding machine paper.

In 1905, the first pizza shop was opened in New York City by Gennaro Lombardini. Mr. Lombardini helped make pizza popular in the United States.

A thousand years ago the Greeks baked oil, vegetables, and olives on flat, round bread dough. They ate this Greek pizza for breakfast.

Today pizza is one of the most popular foods in America and around the world. Some people even like to eat cold pizza for breakfast!

Hundreds of years ago the Spanish brought tomatoes to Italy. At first, most people did not want to eat the strange vegetable. They thought tomatoes were poisonous. Now tomato sauce is an important part of pizza making!

In 1889 Rafaele Esposito was asked to make a special pizza for the queen of Italy, Queen Margherita. He created a pizza that looked like the Italian flag— red tomatoes, green basil, and white mozzarella cheese.

That's an Italian Fact!

tlayl _____ is a long,

otob_____-shaped country in

the Mediterranean Sea.

ylciiS_____ and Sardinia, two

islands, are also a part of Italy. Italy's

capital city is meRo_____. The oosClmues_____ and

rumoF_____ are famous landmarks in Rome. The home of the

cCothali_____ Church, Vatican City, is inside Rome. Both

Rome and Italy have been the home of many famous

rsstait_____ and iasmsunic_____. Another famous

Italian city is nieVec_____. This city is really a group of

ssndali_____. Venice has slaanc_____ instead of roads,

so people travel by oatb_____ instead of cars. Italy has three

famous volcanoes named Mount atnE_____, ntouM_____

Vesuvius, and Mount rtSbmoilo_____.

Word Bank

Venice	Etna	Forum	Rome
musicians	Colosseum	Mount	Stromboli
Catholic	islands	canals	boot
Sicily	Italy	artists	boat

Spaghetti Name Tag

Materials

- dry thin spaghetti
- dry alphabet noodles
- tagboard scraps
- scissors
- hole punch
- glue
- yarn

Directions

1. Cut a house-shaped piece of tagboard using pattern provided at right. Punch a hole in the roof with the hole punch.

2. Glue the spaghetti to the surface of the tagboard (for the roof, lay noodles horizontally; for the house, lay noodles vertically) by spreading a thin layer of glue over the entire surface of the tagboard; allow to dry.

3. If desired, first color the alphabet noodles according to the directions on page 38. Select alphabet noodles to spell Strega Nona (or a child's name) and glue the letters to the front of the spaghetti house; allow to dry.

4. Cut an appropriate length of yarn, loop it through the hole, match the ends, and tie the two ends in a knot to make a name tag necklace.

House Pattern

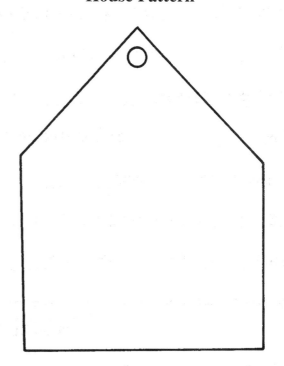

Note: You can adapt the spaghetti name tag to be worn as a pin. Do not create a hole in the house's roof (Step 1). After completing the name tag (Step 3), apply a purchased pinback (available at craft stores) to the back side of the house-shaped tagboard using craft glue or a glue gun.

Pasta and Pizza Plates

Materials

- a supply of 9" (23 cm) paper plates
- colored scrap paper
- natural colored raffia, twine, or string
- scissors
- glue

Directions

1. Encourage the children to think of the visual detail in a piece of pizza or plate of pasta. Discuss the colors and shapes of the different ingredients. (If possible, show colorful pictures of both slices of pizza and plates of sauce-laden pasta.)

2. Provide each child with a paper plate. Have each child use the scrap paper, raffia, twine, or string, scissors, and glue to create a plate of pizza or pasta from the "bottom" up.

Italian Flag

Materials

- 4" x 2" (10 cm x 5 cm) pre-cut red and green construction paper
- 4" x 6" (10 cm x 15 cm) pre-cut white construction paper
- glue
- plastic drinking straw

Directions

1. Glue the green sheet of paper on top of the white sheet of paper, matching up the 4" (10 cm) *left* side edges; allow to dry.

2. Glue the red sheet of paper on top of the white sheet of paper, matching up the 4" (10 cm) *right* side edges; allow to dry.

3. Glue the straw to the *left* side edge of the flag to form a flag pole; allow to dry.

Painting with Pasta

Materials

- 3" (8 cm) lengths of dry string pasta (such as spaghetti or vermicelli)
- dry shaped pasta (farfelle, rotelle, rigatoni, etc.)
- several colors of tempera paints
- shoebox lid
- white paper (cut to fit the inside dimension of the shoebox lid)

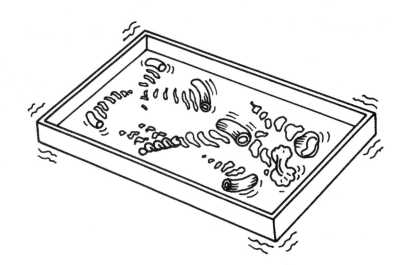

Directions

1. Lay the white paper inside the shoebox lid.

2. Pour a few drops of the chosen paint colors onto the white paper.

3. Place a variety of dry pasta noodles on top of the paint-spotted white paper.

4. Shake the lid side-to-side so that the pasta pieces move around and drag the paint to create the pasta painting. You may add more paint, as well as use additional pasta pieces, if desired.

5. When the desired look is achieved, carefully remove the pasta pieces and white paper from the shoebox lid; allow pasta painting to dry thoroughly.

Pasta Collage

Materials

- dry pasta (try to use as many different shapes as possible)
- 8½" x 11" (22 cm x 28 cm) white cardstock paper
- glue
- gold or silver spray paint
- newspaper

Directions

1. Create a pasta collage design by gluing the pasta pieces to a sheet of white cardstock paper; allow to dry.

2. Place the pasta collage in the center of a portion of spread-out newspaper. Spray the collage with the spray paint; allow to dry.

Pasta and Pizza Songs

Writing your own song is easy. Just choose a tune that you know and change the words. Finish the songs below. Then pick a tune and write one of your own.

(Sung to the tune of *Twinkle, Twinkle, Little Star*)

Pasta's _____, pasta's _____,

I think pasta is _____.

It tastes best when_____.

_____ is my favorite kind.

Pasta's _____, pasta's _____,

I think pasta is really _____.

(Sung to the tune of *Mary Had a Little Lamb*)

_____ had a _____pizza,
(Write your name.)

_____ pizza, _____pizza.

_____ had a _____pizza,
(Write your name.)

and it was _____.

Now it's time for you to make up your own pasta or pizza song using a familiar tune that you know. Write the name of the tune you will use on the line below and write the verse or verses to your song on the back of this paper.

My tune is

_____

Recipes

These pasta and pizza recipes are easy to make and fun to eat. The serving sizes indicate sample-size servings, not meal-size portions.

Quick Pizza

Ingredients

- 8 English muffin or bagel halves
- 1 cup (225 g) shredded mozzarella cheese
- $^3/_4$ cup (180 mL) pizza sauce

Utensils

- cheese grater
- measuring cup
- baking sheet
- tablespoon

Directions

Preheat oven to 450° F (230° C). Place each muffin or bagel half on the baking sheet and top with one tablespoon (15 mL) of pizza sauce. Sprinkle each half with some of the shredded cheese. Bake for 10 minutes or until the cheese has melted. Serves 8.

Pizza Snacks

Ingredients

- 20 whole grain crackers
- 20 pepperoni slices
- $^1/_2$ cup (120 mL) pizza sauce
- 1 cup (225 g) shredded parmesan or mozzarella cheese

Utensils

- teaspoon
- measuring cup
- three paper plates

Directions

Spread one teaspoon (5 mL) of pizza sauce onto each cracker. Top each cracker with a pinch of cheese and a pepperoni slice. Divide the pizza crackers and place them onto the three paper plates. Microwave the crackers for about 20 seconds on high. Serves 20.

Dessert Pizza

Ingredients

- $^1/_2$ cup (100 g) brown sugar
- $^1/_2$ cup (100 g) softened butter
- 1 teaspoon (5 mL) vanilla
- $^1/_2$ cup (100 g) quick-cook oatmeal
- $^1/_2$ cup (100 g) flaked coconut
- 1 cup (225 g) chopped nuts
- 1 cup (225 g) candy-coated chocolate pieces
- $^1/_3$ cup (75 g) granulated sugar
- 1 egg
- 1 cup (225 g) all-purpose flour
- $^1/_2$ teaspoon (2.5 mL) baking soda
- 1 cup (225 g) semisweet chocolate chips
- 1 can (16 ounces/450 g) vanilla frosting

Recipes *(cont.)*

Dessert Pizza *(cont.)*

Utensils

- measuring cups
- mixing spoon
- teaspoon
- knife
- large bowl
- 12" (30 cm) pizza pan

Directions

Preheat oven to 350° F (180° C). In a large bowl, mix the sugars, butter, egg, and vanilla until combined thoroughly. Add the flour, baking soda, and oatmeal; mix well (the dough will be stiff). Fold in the chocolate chips. Spread the dough evenly over the area of the pizza pan and bake 10 to 12 minutes, or until dough appears golden brown. Remove the cookie and cool completely. Spread the frosting to almost the edge of the cookie, leaving a "crust" appearance. Sprinkle on the coconut, chocolate candy pieces, and nuts. Cut the dessert pizza into 16 pizza slices.

Speedy Macaroni and Cheese

Ingredients

- 1 cup (225 g) elbow macaroni
- 1 cup (240 mL) milk
- 1/4 cup (50 g) margarine
- 1 cup (225 g) shredded American cheese

Utensils

- measuring cup
- pasta pot
- colander
- large spoon

Directions

Cook the macaroni according to the package directions; drain. Place macaroni back into the empty pasta pot. Stir in the margarine, milk, and cheese. Cook the macaroni and cheese over low heat for about five minutes, stirring frequently. Makes 10 to 12 servings.

Easy Pasta Salad

Ingredients

- 2 cups (450 g) rotini or ziti pasta, cooked
- 1 medium zucchini
- 1 cup (240 mL) bottled Italian salad dressing
- 1/2 cup (100 g) pepperoni
- 2 carrots
- 1 green pepper

Utensils

- knife
- measuring cup
- large bowl
- mixing spoon

Directions

Cut the pepperoni, carrots, zucchini, and green pepper into bite size-pieces. Add to the cooked pasta. Pour in the salad dressing; mix thoroughly. Chill the salad. Serves 20.

Recipes *(cont.)*

German Spaetzle

Ingredients

- 1 cup (225 g) flour
- 2 tablespoons (30 mL) water
- 1 egg
- 2 tablespoons (28 g) butter
- pinch of salt

Utensils

- measuring cup
- spatula
- tablespoon
- pasta pot
- large bowl
- strainer
- wooden spoon

Directions

Pour the flour into the bowl. Make a well in the center of the flour; break the egg into the well. Add the salt and water. Mix into a smooth elastic paste with the spoon (adding more water, if necessary). Lift out the dough and place it on a lightly floured flat surface. Knead the dough for two to three minutes. Using the spatula, cut off small pieces of the spaetzle dough (about the size of a large grape), roll the dough into a small thick rope, and drop the dough into the pasta pot filled with boiling water. Cook until tender (about two minutes), drain, place back into the empty pasta pot, and add the butter. Toss gently to melt the butter. Serves 20.

Greek Orzo Salad

Ingredients

- 1 cup (225 g) uncooked orzo (rice-shaped pasta)
- $\frac{1}{2}$ teaspoon (2.5 mL) grated lemon peel
- 1 tablespoon (15 mL) olive oil
- 1 cup (225 g) chopped tomato
- 15 pitted olives, chopped
- $\frac{1}{2}$ cup (100 g) crumbled feta cheese
- juice of one lemon
- 1 tablespoon (15 mL) honey
- $\frac{1}{2}$ tablespoon (8 mL) spicy mustard
- 1 cup (225 g) chopped zucchini
- $\frac{1}{4}$ cup (50 g) chopped fresh mint leaves

Utensils

- measuring cup
- measuring spoons
- pasta pot
- large bowl
- strainer
- wire whisk
- small bowl
- mixing spoon

Directions

Cook the orzo according to the packaged directions, drain, rinse with cold water, and set aside. In the small bowl, blend the lemon juice, lemon peel, olive oil, honey, and mustard with the wire whisk. In the large bowl, add the cooked orzo, chopped ingredients, and dressing; combine with the mixing spoon. Sprinkle the salad with the feta cheese and serve. Makes 20 servings.

Dancing Noodle Necklace

Preparation

Refer to page 38 to create a variety of colored dry pasta. **Note:** The dried pasta used for the noodle necklaces must be able to be stringed, such as macaroni or penne noodles.

Directions for Necklace

Using yarn, string, dental floss, or fishing line, have your children string the colored pasta using a repetitive color pattern. (**Note:** The initial core color pattern should be repeated two additional times. For example: blue, blue, red, red, red, green, green; blue, blue, red, red, red, green, green; blue, blue, red, red, red, green, green).

Directions for Noodle Dance

Assign a movement for each color of dyed pasta. For example, blue = jump with both legs, red = skip on one leg, and green = hop on one foot. Using the colored noodle pattern described above, the noodle necklace dance would be jump, jump, skip, skip, skip, hop, hop, jump, jump, skip, skip, skip, hop, hop, jump, jump, skip, skip, skip, hop, hop. After the children dance their own noodle necklace dances, have them trade noodle necklaces and dance one another's color patterns.

Pasta Relay Race

Materials

- masking tape or string
- 3 soup ladles
- 3 pasta pots
- 3 bowls
- 6 chairs
- 6 pounds (3 kg) uncooked macaroni
- one-cup (225 g) measuring cup

Directions

Determine a start and finish line; mark the lines with tape or string. Place three chairs side-by-side behind the starting line and place the three remaining chairs side-by-side behind the finishing line (seats of the chairs will act as tabletops). Divide the macaroni evenly between the three large bowls. Place one ladle in each of the macaroni-filled bowls. Place one of the prepared bowls on each of the three starting-line chairs. On the three finish-line chairs, place the empty pasta pots.

Organize your children into three teams. Have the children line up behind the bowls of macaroni. At the sound of a starting signal, the first child on each team scoops up a ladleful of noodles and runs to the finishing line to place the noodles into his or her team's pasta pot. The child then runs back to the starting line and hands the ladle to his or her next team member. The relay continues until one team has had all their team players complete the relay. The winning team is determined by measuring the final amount of pasta in each finish-line bowl using the measuring cup. The team with the most pasta wins.

Web Sites

The Web sites listed below will prove helpful in gaining information, recipes, nutritional facts, and children's activity sheets to enhance your pasta and pizza unit.

Ragu (Mama's Cucina)
http://www.ragu.com

This site is set up to simulate a visit through Mama's home. You can visit her kitchen and dining room, meet the family (staff at Ragu), read and print out Mama's recipes from *Mama's Secrets* cookbook, talk to Mama, and sign up for the Ragu newsletter.

Pizza Hut
http://www.pizzahut.com

This Web site is advertisement-based, but still may be of interest to you if you would like to know what Pizza Hut's latest campaigns are and learn what their new pizza specialties will be.

Rosetto's Pasta
http://www.rosetto.com

You will be greeted by Albert Giuseppe, called "Al Dente" by his friends. You can explore Al's kitchen for his secret recipes, print out games and activities for the bambinis (children), and find out if Rosetto cooking classes are being offered in your geographical area.

The Tomato Page
http://www.tomato.org

Here you will find tomato tips from the California Tomato Commission along with interesting tomato facts, nutritional profiles, recipes, and tomato Web site links.

Domino's
http://www.dominos.com

This site is advertisement-based and mainly lets you know the closest Domino's take-out location(s).

Mueller's Pasta
http://www.cpcinternational.com/profile_history_muellers.htm

At this Web site you will find a brief history of pasta as well as the history of Mueller's Pasta. Links to other Best Foods (parent company of Mueller's) product sites and company profiles are also available.

Operetta Extravaganza!

Conclude your pasta and pizza unit with an edible and audible celebration! An operetta performance and tasty pasta and pizza treats will prove fun-filled for all those invited.

Invitations

Invite your guests by having your children create invitations using the pizza slice pattern on page 33. Reproduce copies of the pizza slice onto tan-colored paper and have the children cut out the pizza slices. On the slices' cover (the outside blank portion of the foldable slices), have the children write *Operetta Extravaganza!* with crayons or markers. On the inside lines, have the children write the date (give yourself one to two weeks to allow for preparing and practicing the operetta), time, and place where the extravaganza will be held. Complete the invitations by having the children color the slices' covers to reflect pizza slices with toppings.

Planning Time

Begin to plan the extravaganza with your children. You will need to decide on background music, refreshments, seating for the guests, the operetta stage area design, props for the operetta, and how to divide up the roles and duties for performing the operetta (page 65).

The Big Day

As your guests arrive, have an opera recording playing softly in the background, such as *La Boheme, Tosca, Aida, Rigoletto*, or *La Traviata* (opera recordings can be found at most local libraries or music stores). Have appointed children greet the guests and escort them to the seating area (centered in front of the operetta stage area). Have the greeters give the guests copies of the operetta song finale sheet (page 69) and tell the guests that the operetta will begin shortly.

When ready to start the performance, have an assigned child introduce the operetta by first sharing a little background information on opera history (page 65) and then give a brief background of the operetta's storyline.

Refreshments

It is suggested that you serve refreshments after the operetta performance. In a prepared area, have all of the eating utensils, plates, cups, and napkins needed for serving the refreshments. An appropriate food, given the nature of the operetta, would be Pizza Margherita (page 26) or you may use one or more of the pasta and pizza recipes found on pages 59 to 61. Serve white or red grape juice as "Italian wine."

Memories

After the guests have enjoyed their refreshments, thank them for attending the extravaganza and have the children present each guest with a special gift as a memento such as spaghetti name tags (page 55), Italian flags (page 56), pasta collages (page 57), or noodle necklaces (page 62). If you would prefer a simpler memento, hand out prepared awards (page 77).

Preparing the Operetta

Background Knowledge

Italy has contributed much to art and music throughout history. It is said that the first opera, *Dafne,* was written in Florence, Italy, in 1597. An opera is a play with text set to music and sung with an orchestral accompaniment. An operetta is a short, amusing musical play. An opera or operetta may contain both singing and spoken lines. (If possible, have your children listen to an Italian opera recording and show them pictures of an opera stage production before you begin planning the operetta.)

Let The Planning Begin

The focus of the operetta, *Pizza Fit For a Queen,* is a retelling of the story shared in the children's mini-book featured on pages 22 to 26. To begin the planning process, divide the children into actors, costumers, set designers, sound effect team members, and musicians.

Actors

You may hold auditions, or simply choose the three lead actors. You will need two boys (Rafaele, pronounced "Ra-fay-Ela," and Marcello, pronounced "Mar-CHel-o") and one girl (Queen Margherita, pronounced "Mar-ger-Ee-ta" [hard *g* sound]). You will also need to select five to ten children to be the townspeople.

Costumers

The costuming period for the operetta is in the late 1800s in Naples, Italy. You will need a chef's hat and apron for Rafaele, a mustache and gentleman's period costume for Marcello, and a long fancy gown and crown for Queen Margherita. You will also need commoners' period costumes for the townspeople. The costumers may also choose to add details such as mustaches and beards to the male townspeople.

Set Designers

Your set designers are responsible for the operetta's scenery and props. They will need to create or assemble the pizzeria background (two empty refrigerator boxes, split open, with a scene depicting the inside walls of the pizzeria drawn or painted on the boxes' panels work well) as well as the interior of the pizzeria (two to three tables covered with red-and-white-checked tablecloths and accompanying chairs), a cookbook, tomatoes, basil leaves, a chunk of mozzarella cheese, a grocery bag, cooking utensils, a baked Queen Margherita pizza (page 26) that has been cut into small pieces (but still looks like an uncut pizza), eating utensils, napkins, and paper dinner plates.

Sound Effects

The sound effects team will need to create the necessary sounds for the operetta. They will need to study the operetta's script (pages 66 to 68) to determine what sounds need to be made (for example, an "opening door" sound as Rafaele enters his pizzeria).

Musicians

The musicians may work with a music teacher (if available) or another musically-inclined adult to prepare accompaniment for the singing using rhythm instruments or a keyboard. Simple melodies can be created using only the black keys at the center of the keyboard (pentatonic scale). **Note:** The songs can be sung acappella if no musical instruments or musically-inclined adults are available to assist.

Operetta

Scene One

Outside the pizzeria. Rafaele, wearing a chef's hat and apron is about to enter his pizzeria when Marcello approaches him. Marcello sings to the tune of *Row, Row, Row Your Boat:*

Oh, my Rafaele,

have you heard the news?

Queen Margherita wants to eat some pizza

to take away her blues.

Hurry, my good friend.

You must do your best.

Create a brand new kind of pizza

for your honored guest!

Scene Two

Marcello and Rafaele enter the pizzeria and stand near a table that has a cookbook laying on it. Rafaele looks in the cookbook and then sings to the tune of *Farmer in the Dell:*

Pizza for the Queen,

pizza for the Queen.

Oh, what must I buy to make

a Pizza for the Queen?

I'll need red tomatoes,

and mozzarella, too.

A chewy crust and basil green.

A pizza for the Queen!

Scene Three

Rafaele exits the pizzeria. He returns immediately and re-enters the pizzeria carrying a bag of groceries and begins preparing a pizza.

Marcello asks: **"What are you making, my friend?"**

Operetta *(cont.)*

Scene Three *(cont.)*

Rafaele answers, **"I must make a pizza like no other, the best pizza in all of Naples, for Queen Margherita. My pizza will be a picture of our Italian flag. For red, I will use these tomatoes** *(shows Marcello the tomatoes)* **and for green I will use fresh basil leaves."** *(Shows and smells the basil leaves.)*

Marcello asks, **"That is very good, my friend, but what will make the white of our flag?"**

Rafaele answers, **"I have thought about that.** *(Shows Marcello the cheese.)* **Here is some mozzarella cheese. That will be the white of our country's flag."**

Marcello says excitedly, **"Bella, pizza! Bella, Rafaele! You have created a masterpiece!"**

Marcello exits the pizzeria. Rafaele continues to work on the pizza.

Scene Four

One of the tables in the pizzeria is set with a fork, knife, napkin, paper plates, and the baked Queen Margherita pizza. Rafaele and Marcello are waiting for the queen. She enters and sits down. Rafaele presents her with his pizza *(holding it up slightly so audience can see how it has been designed)*. She tastes a piece of the pizza and then sings to the tune of *Three Blind Mice*:

My, oh my,
I love this pizza pie.
Rafaele has made the best!
This surely is a pizza-fest!
Red, white and green are what we see
upon the flag of Italy!
My, oh my,
I love this pizza pie!

Operetta (cont.)

Scene Four (cont.)

Queen Margherita motions to the townspeople who are waiting just outside to enter the pizzeria. She continues singing to the tune of *Three Blind Mice:*

**Dear people of the town,
come in and sit down.
I want you all to have a treat
of a pizza that is really neat.
Topped with cheese, it's sure to please.
My, oh my,
I love this pizza pie!**

Rafaele passes out small pieces of the pizza to all of the townspeople on paper plates. They taste it, smile, and begin whispering to one another. They then all hold up their pizza pieces as a salute to Rafaele and sing to the tune of *Old MacDonald had a Farm:*

**(Queen solo) This pizza is the best I've seen!
(All) Bravo, Rafaele!
(Rafaele) I made it special for my Queen.
(All) Bravo, Rafaele!
(All) There's chewy crust here, and tasty sauce there.
Chewy crust, tasty sauce, it's such a special treat!
(Queen solo) This pizza is the best in town!
(All) Bravo, Rafaele!**

Rafaele bows low before the queen. Queen Margherita turns to the audience and asks the guests to sing along with her and the townspeople in honor of Raphaele. *(The audience have been given copies of the words to the operetta song finale.)*

Sing the finale.

The actors and townspeople hold hands and bow to the audience. This concludes the operetta performance.

Operetta Song Finale

Sung to the tune of *Old MacDonald had a Farm.*

  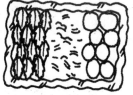

(Queen solo)
This pizza is the best I've seen!

(Everyone)
Bravo, Rafaele!

(Rafaele)
I made it special for my Queen.

(Everyone)
Bravo, Rafaele!

(Everyone)
There's chewy crust here,
and tasty sauce there.
Chewy crust, tasty sauce,
it's such a special treat!

(Queen solo)
This pizza is the best in town!

(Everyone)
Bravo, Rafaele!

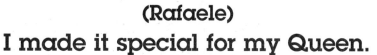
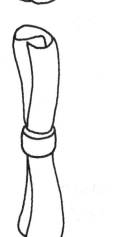
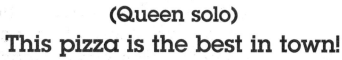

Bulletin Board Ideas

An Italian Look

Cover a bulletin-board background area with paper. Enlarge the map of Italy (page 71) using a copying machine with enlarging capabilities or by making a transparency of the map and using an overhead projector to project the map onto bulletin-board or chart paper and tracing the illustrations and text. Attach the created map to the bulletin-board background. Mark the cities of Rome, Naples, and Calabria with small flag markers made from construction paper and toothpicks. To the left of the map, on a large sheet of paper, list the recipe (ingredients and directions) for preparing spaghetti. To the right of the map, also on a large sheet of paper, list the recipe for pizza by writing out your favorite recipe.

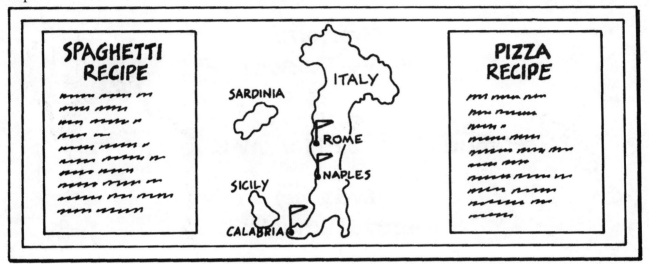

Is it Good for You?

Add to a covered bulletin-board area a collage of actual empty packages or labels showing the nutritional facts for a variety of pasta and pizza food items, such as tomato and alfredo pasta sauces, dried pasta, packaged or frozen pizzas, and canned pasta. (If feasible, have your children collect and donate their own food labels to the bulletin board's collage.) Enlarge the nutritional portions of some of the labels onto construction paper and attach them to the bulletin board. Encourage the children to read the labels' nutritional facts. Then have them make comparisons of the items' calories, fat grams, and sodium contents.

Map of Italy

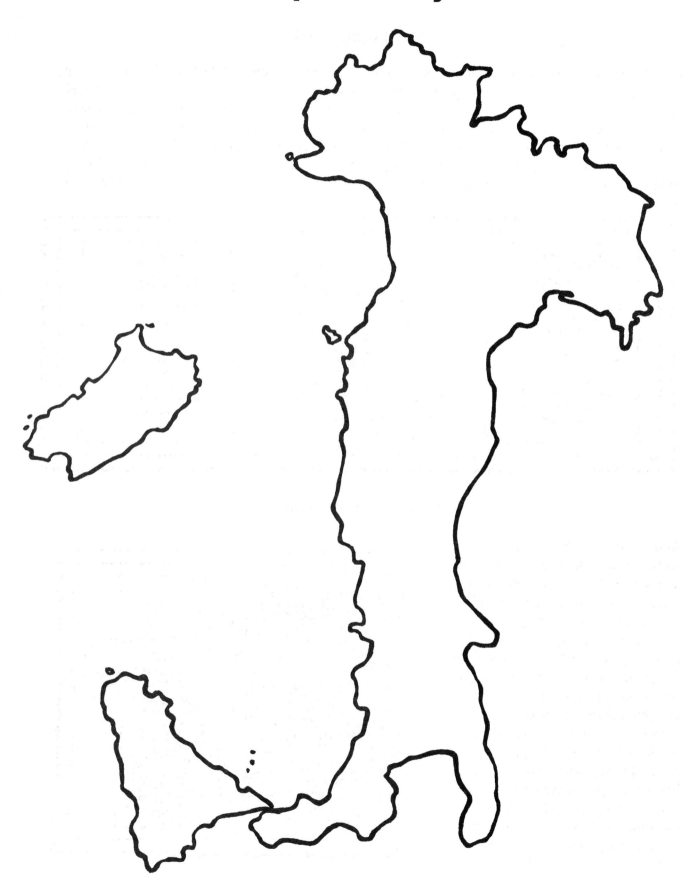

Learning Centers

A learning center is a special area set aside for the study or review of a specific skill or topic. Centers can be designed for use by individuals or small groups of children.

Reading

Start by placing pasta- and pizza-related newspaper, magazine advertisements and/or recipes, and standard cookbooks in the center area. Add a collection of fiction and nonfiction books about pasta and pizza (Bibliography, page 79). Children especially enjoy listening to story recordings read by parents or other family members, as well as by people who are important to their lives, such as you, the school principal, librarian, custodian, and so on. You may want to arrange for some of these special people to tape record popular pasta- and pizza-based stories (Bibliography, page 79) for use in the listening center. If possible, provide multiple copies of the recorded stories so that the children can follow along textually as they are listening to the stories. A wonderful alternative to listening to an audio tape is to have a "live" guest reader come in and read to the children in small groups. The children can then retell the story to the guest reader utilizing a pocket chart (page 31) and pre-written sentence strips that sequence the story's text.

Math

Provide a large amount of dry pasta shapes to be used for free exploration or planned counting and sorting activities. Younger children can simply sort the pasta by shape or create a pasta pattern (page 38). They can also practice one-to-one correspondence by placing the correct number of dry pasta pieces onto prepared number word cards. Older children can practice counting pasta shapes in groups of twos, fives, tens, and so on.

Another fun activity is to have the children estimate the number of pasta shells in a jar. Prepare for this estimation activity by placing two same-size jars in the center area. In one of the jars place only ten of the chosen pasta shapes; fill the other jar completely full of dried pasta. Have the children make estimation predictions by first focusing on what ten pasta shapes look like in one jar, then predicting the total amount of dry pasta in the filled-up jar.

For fraction practice, provide brown cardboard circles (often times pizza restaurants will give you cardboard circles for free or at a low cost) "covered" with red sauce (drawn with red permanent markers or paint) and a container of pre-cut paper pizza toppings. Children demonstrate an understanding of fractions by placing orders with a partner. One child might tell his or her partner, who is acting as the pizza chef, "I'd like my pizza to have one-half pepperoni, one-fourth mushrooms, and one-fourth green peppers." The partner then places the fractional amounts onto the pizza-sauced circle using the appropriate amount of paper toppings.

Science

Place this center near a sunny window. Grow tomato seedlings, herb plants, or onion bulbs. Have the children keep daily science journals recording the growth and care of their plants.

Learning Centers *(cont.)*

Pizza Game

The educational goal of this game is to aid in reinforcing learned pasta and pizza knowledge gained during this thematic unit. Reproduce four pizza gameboards (page 74) onto light-brown tagboard. Color in the sauce areas with either a red pencil or permanent red marker. Cut out the gameboards around the crusts' edges; laminate the gameboards for durability. Reproduce the true and false pizza gamecard statements (pages 75–76) by cutting out forty-two 2 ³/₄" (7 cm) diameter circles from tan construction paper to represent pepperoni slices. On one side of a cut out circle, copy one of the statements and its appropriate answer, true or false, on the backside of the circle. Repeat the process using the remaining forty-one circles.

To play the pizza game, each player gets a pizza gameboard and places it in front of himself or herself as if the gameboard was a place mat. The pepperoni statement circles are randomly mixed and placed between the players in an empty lunch-size bag or a pizza delivery box. One child is designated to be first. The child sitting to his or her immediate left (if more than two players are playing) pulls out one of the pepperoni statement circles from the bag or box and reads the statement. The questioned child answers "true" or "false." If the answer given is correct, the child is given the pepperoni statement circle and places it on his or her pizza gameboard. If answered incorrectly, the pizza statement circle goes back into the bag or box. The child who just read the statement circle is now the one who listens to a statement circle being read by the child sitting to his or her left. The game continues in this fashion until all of the statement circles have been answered correctly and are on the players' pizza gameboards. The children then count up their own statement circles. The winner is one with the most pepperoni "slices."

Note: Your children can make up their own true and false statements and record them on prepared blank "pepperoni" statement circles.

Pizza Gameboard

Pizza Gamecard Statements

See page 73 for suggested use.

The first American pizzeria was in Chicago. **False** (New York)

The first pizzeria in the USA was in New York City. **True**

Queen Margherita is the name of a kind of pizza. **True**

Pizza Margherita has pepperoni on it. **False** (tomato, mozzarella cheese, and basil)

Pizza Margherita was created in 1889. **True**

Queen Margherita visited a pizzeria in Naples, Italy. **True**

Rafaele Esposito created a pizza for Queen Margherita. **True**

Strega Nona and Big Anthony lived in Calabria, Italy. **True**

Strega Nona hired Big Anothony to help her with chores. **True**

Strega Nona blew 2 kisses in her pot to stop it boiling. **False** (3 kisses)

Big Anthony obeyed Strega Nona. **False** (He used her pasta pot.)

Big Anthony threw all the pasta in the river. **False** (He ate it.)

Pasta is made from flour, water, and eggs. **True**

Pasta comes in many shapes and sizes. **True**

People in Asian countries eat pasta. **True**

Australian people like eggs on their pizza. **True**

People from Brazil like chicken on their pizza. **False** (green peas)

People from England like tuna and corn on their pizza. **True**

Christopher Columbus brought pasta to Italy. **False** (Marco Polo)

Pasta can be purchased fresh or dried. **True**

Pasta is cooked in boiling water. **True**

Pizza Gamecard Statements *(cont.)*

See page 73 for suggested use.

Tomatoes are a good source of vitamins A and C. **True**

People used to believe tomatoes were poisonous. **True**

Tomatoes are mostly made of fat. **False** (water)

Pizza dough rises because it is made with flour. **False** (yeast)

Pizza is baked in a cold oven. **False** (hot)

The Italian flag colors are red, white, and blue. **False** (red, white, and green)

Someone or something from Italy is called Italian. **True**

An Italian pizza baker is called a pizzaiolo. **True**

Italy is shaped like a house. **False** (a boot)

Italy is a city. **False** (a country)

Rome is the capital of Italy. **True**

Vatican City is the home of the Catholic Church. **True**

The Colosseum is in Venice. **False** (Rome)

Venice is a city that is a group of islands. **True**

In Venice, people mainly drive cars on roads. **False** (ride boats through the canals)

Mount Vesuvius is in Italy. **True**

Sicily and Sardinia are islands. **True**

The color of mozzarella cheese is yellow. **False** (white)

Fresh herbs are sometimes used as medicine. **True**

Pizza Hut was started in 1958. **True**

Pizza Hut was first located in New York. **False** (Kansas)

Awards

You add
PIZZA-Z

to
our class!
We're glad you are here!

_____   _____
Teacher   Date

You are showing great pasta-bilities in

_____

Bravo!

_____   _____
Teacher   Date

Thanks for Helping!

We will be starting a pasta and pizza thematic unit soon. If possible, could you help by sending in any of the following items? Please send in your selected items by _____.

date

- a package of elbow macaroni
- a package of spaghetti
- a package of shaped pasta
- a jar of spaghetti sauce
- a jar of alfredo sauce
- a jar of pizza sauce
- a package of mozzarella cheese
- a package of parmesan cheese

- English muffins
- plain crackers
- wheat crackers
- plain bagels
- small cups
- paper plates
- plastic forks
- plastic spoons

Also, if you can help during the cooking experiences, please let me know. Fill in the bottom portion of this note and return it tomorrow.

Grazie,

✄ -

I can provide these items:

_____

_____

_____ Yes, I can help in the classroom. I can help you on these days and at these times: _____

_____

Please call me at _____ to make arrangements.

Signed _____ Date _____

Bibliography

Fiction

Barbour, Karen. *Little Nino's Pizzeria.* HBJ, 1987.

Bastyra, Judy. *Pizza Fun.* Kingfisher, 1997.

dePaola, Tomie. *Big Anthony: His Story.* Putnam, 1998.

dePaola, Tomie. *Strega Nona: Her Story.* Putnam, 1996.

Kovalski, Maryann. *Pizza For Breakfast.* Morrow Junior, 1991.

MacCarone, Grace. *Pizza Party.* Cartwheel, 1994.

Martino, Teresa. *Pizza!* Raintree, 1989.

Murray, Peter. *The Perfect Pizza.* Child's World, 1997.

Pelham, David. *Sam's Pizza: Your Pizza to Go.* Dutton, 1996.

Rey, Margaret. *Curious George and the Pizza.* Houghton Mifflin, 1985.

Robinson, Fay. *Pizza Soup.* Children's Book Press, 1993.

Sanzari. Sylvester. *The King of Pizza: A Magical Story About the World's Largest Pizza.* Workman Publishing, 1995.

Steig, William. *Pete's Pizza.* HarperCollins, 1998.

Walter, Virginia. *Hi Pizza Man.* Orchard, 1998.

Weeks, Sara. *Noodles.* HarperCollins, 1996.

Nonfiction

Angelillo, Barbara Walsh. *Italy.* Steck-Vaughn Library, 1991.

Buck-Murray, Marion. *Kids Make Pizza.* Prima Publishing, 1995.

Calgon, Dorothy. *Pizza All Around.* Parachute, 1992.

Corey, Melinda. *Let's Visit a Spaghetti Factory.* Troll, 1990.

Egan, Robert. *From Wheat to Pasta.* Children's Press, 1997.

Haskins, Jim. *Count Your Way Through Italy.* Carolrhoda, 1990.

Haycock, Kate. *Pasta.* Carolrhoda, 1991.

Krensky, Steven. *All the Pizza Book.* Scholastic, 1992.

MacHotka, Hana. *Pasta Factory.* Houghton Mifflin, 1992.

Martino, Teresa. *Pizza.* Steck-Vaughn, 1998.

Pillar, Marjorie. *Pizza Man.* T.Y. Crowell, 1990.

Peterson, Cris. *Extra Cheese, Please.* Boyds Mills, 1994.

Powell, Jillian. *Italy.* Bookwright Press, 1992.

Powell, Jillian. *Pasta (Everyone Eats).* Raintree, 1997.

Ridgwell, Jenny. *A Taste of Italy.* Thomson Learning, 1993.

Rotner, Shelley. *Hold the Anchovies!* Orchard, 1996.

Stein, R. Conrad. *Italy.* Children's Press, 1984.

Thomson, Peggy. *Siggy's Spaghetti Works.* Tambourine, 1993.

Watt, Fiona. *Pasta and Pizza for Beginners.* EDC Publications, 1998.

Teacher Created Materials

TCM 436 *Strega Nona* Literature Unit

Book It!

For information about *Book It!*, Pizza Hut's national reading incentive program, contact Pizza Hut Incorporated, 1481 Dallas Parkway, Dallas, Texas 75240-2100. 1-800-426-6548.

Pizza Math Game

Pizza Party. Ideal. Product Number 7743. This game is housed in an approved Pizza Hut pizza box and contains two spinners, activity sheets, 59 full-color fraction pizza pieces, and directions for playing the game.

Answer Key

Page 14 From Factory to Store
1. Wheat fields
2. Wheat harvested from fields
3. Bags of grain
4. Mixing and kneading machine
5. Cutting machine
6. Drying rack
7. Package of pasta
8. Pasta packages on shelves

Page 15 Pasta Around the World
United States—macaroni and cheese (mak-uh-Roh-nee and CH-eez)
Germany—spaetzle (Shpht-sehl)
China—mein (Mayn)
Greece—pastitsio (pah-Steet-see-oh)
Italy—spaghetti (spuh-Geht-ee)
Poland—pierogi (peer-Oh-gee)
Japan—ramen (Rah-mehn)

Page 18 Making Fresh Pasta
1. Measure one cup of flour onto a flat surface.
2. Make a well in the cup of flour.
3. Break one egg into the flour.
4. Use a fork to mix together the flour and egg.
5. Use your hands to knead the pasta dough.
6. Let the dough rest for 15 minutes.
7. Roll the dough out very thin.
8. Cut the dough into the shapes you want.
9. Bring a pot of water to boil.
10. Cook the pasta in boiling water for 1-2 minutes.

Page 37 A Naples Pizzeria
4 punctuation mistakes
  (2 periods missing; 2 sentences ending with question marks should end with periods)
4 capitalization mistakes
  (italy; mount; vesuvius; neapolitan)
6 spelling mistakes
  (piza; Napels; kneeded; tomatos; frech; bee)
1. pizzaiolo—a pizza maker from Naples
2. kneaded—mixed; folding dough with hands
3. Mt. Vesuvius—a volcano
4. Neapolitan—a person from Naples, Italy

Page 43 Is it Time to Eat?
1. 5:00
2. 5:30
3. 4:10
4. 4:30

Page 46 Tomato Sauce
1. Tomato seedlings
2. Tomato plants
3. Harvesting the tomatoes
4. Trucking the tomatoes
5. Vats of tomatoes
6. Canning the tomatoes
7. Loading the delivery truck
8. Tomato cans on shelves

Page 47 Nutritional Facts
1. crust—breads
   pepperoni—meat
   tomato sauce—vegetable
   cheese—dairy
2. macaroni—pasta
   butter—fats or dairy
   cheese—dairy
   milk—dairy
3. spaghetti—pasta
   cheese—dairy
   meat balls—meat
   tomato sauce—vegetable
4. lasagne—pasta
   cheese—dairy
   eggplant—vegetable
   tomato sauce—vegetable

Page 50 A World of Toppings
India—pickled ginger
England—tuna and corn
Russia—sardines, salmon, and onions
Brazil—green peas
Bahamas—barbecued chicken
Unites States—pepperoni
Australia—eggs
Singapore—curried chicken and beef

Page 51 The Story of Pizza Hut
1. Dan and Frank Carney; 1958
2. Wichita, Kansas
3. thin crust pizza and drinks
4. salads and sandwiches
5. Kentucky Fried Chicken and Taco Bell